By Diane Wolkstein

THE COOL RIDE IN THE SKY

SQUIRREL'S SONG

THE VISIT

8,000 STONES

LAZY STORIES

THE RED LION

THE MAGIC ORANGE TREE
and Other Haitian Folktales

The Magic Orange Tree

And Other Haitian Folktales

Collected by
DIANE WOLKSTEIN

Drawings by
ELSA HENRIQUEZ

Schocken Books ● New York

Library of Congress Cataloging in Publication Data
Wolkstein, Diane.
  The magic orange tree, and other Haitian folktales.

  Reprint of the 1978 ed. published by Knopf, New York.
  SUMMARY: A collection of folktales gathered by the
author in Haiti with comments on Haitian folklore.
  1. Tales, Haitian. [1. Folklore—Haiti]
I. Henriquez, Elsa. II. Title.
[PZ8.1.W84Mag 1980]   398.2'097294   79-22787
ISBN 0-8052-0650-7

Book design by Tony DeLuna

Manufactured in the United States of America
9 8 7 6

First SCHOCKEN edition published in 1980

Contents

The Magic Orange Tree

And Other
Haitian Folktales

Introduction

"*Cric?*"* the Haitian storyteller calls out when she or he has a story to tell. "*Crac!*"* the audience responds *if* they want that storyteller to begin. If they do not respond with *crac!*, the storyteller cannot begin. "*Cric?*" another storyteller calls out, hoping for the welcoming "*crac!*"

It is not that the audience is rude in refusing one storyteller and choosing another; rather, they are giving their pledge. For if the listeners cry *crac!* they are expected to, and do, give their full support to the storyteller. They listen to hear that the story is told correctly. Embellishments are accepted, confusion or losses of memory are not. The listeners comment on the events and characters of the stories. They comment on the storyteller's talents. And as soon as a song begins within a story, the audience joins in. I have heard groups joyously sing the chorus ten and twenty times.

Communal storytelling in Haiti takes place

* *Cric* is pronounced "creek." *Crac* is pronounced "crack." *Cric?-Crac!* an introductory phrase to French stories, is said to have been brought to Haiti by the *Breton* sailors in the seventeenth century.

Since there is still controversy in Haiti concerning the phonetic spellings of Creole words, I have chosen the gallicized spellings. The Frenchified system also permits a certain access to the Creole words to the English- and French-speaking reader.

outside the capital city of Port-au-Prince, in the plains, mountains, and countryside. In these rural areas the men work in the fields and the women take care of the household. Once a week the women sell the family produce in the marketplace. The houses are small thatched-roof huts, without electricity. In the evenings the families create their own entertainment. When the adults are not too tired, and especially when the moon is full or on a Saturday evening, they gather outside on their steps and talk and gossip. Soon a story may be thought of. *Cric?*

In moments a group might gather: friends, neighbors, teen-agers, children, and toddlers. With many ready to tell, the storytellers must compete for a chance. If a storyteller tells well, he will call out *cric?* just as he is finishing his last sentence, but perhaps someone else has already called out *cric?* Then the general sentiment of the crowd decides who will be the one to unwind the magic thread.

Children of seven or eight mouth the words as the storytellers speak, for most of the stories are already well-known. But if the children are too noisy, they will be reprimanded and sent away. Sometimes they will gather at a distance and form their own group, telling stories and imitating the gestures and intonations of the adults.

Though the stories involve set gestures and expressions, what is most exciting is the variety and inventiveness of the individual storyteller. The best storyteller takes a story known to all and creates his or her own story. Everyone knows the tale, but this time what will the storyteller give? in entertainment? in imagery? in wisdom?

Many of the tales I recognized at once because of their European or African counterparts. "Mother of the Waters" is a version of the German "Mother Holle" collected by the Grimm brothers. "Bye-Bye" resembles the Basotho tale "Tortoise and Dove" collected by Minnie Postma. Other stories, such as "The Two Donkeys," "Owl," and "The Last Tiger in Haiti," were new to me. Yet even those stories I had known were different. It was like eating fruit such as apples and pears all your life and suddenly tasting mangoes and papayas and guavas.

Odette Menesson Rigaud and Milo Rigaud who have lived in Haiti for the past forty years and are profoundly involved in Voodoo, the religious life of the peasants, were the ones who introduced me to the fruits of the Haitian night. It was Odette who, in 1971 wrote a letter of introduction to Jean-Baptiste Romain, director of the Faculté d'Ethnologie of the State University of Haiti. He in turn introduced me to the remarkable Jeanne Philippe, a practicing psychoanalyst, country doctor, lover of stories, and child of a Carib Indian mother and Haitian father. Many evenings I sat on the porch of Dr. Philippe's house and listened with Jeanne and her parents to the peasants in the neighborhood tell stories, which the family knew well but loved to hear again. Jeanne's neighbor, Willy, often accompanied me to hear stories in Carrefour-Dufort, a country village fifteen miles southwest of Port-au-Prince. And Odette took me to visit her friends at Croix-des Missions, Diquini, Planton-Café, and Masson.

Before I left for Haiti, I had read of the tradition of the professional storytellers (*maître conte*), who were not paid but offered food and lodging in exchange for their talents. In the eighteenth century, they traveled from one plantation to another and were most often called upon to perform at festivals and wakes. If a child died, they would tell simple stories; if an important man died, long romances. But in the 1920s, most of the master storytellers left Haiti with the other farmers because there was work available cutting sugar cane in Cuba.

On the chance that a few master storytellers might still be in Haiti, I would ask at each storytelling evening if anyone knew a *maître conte*. Almost everyone knew or had known of one who lived in this or that village, always one village or one night away. I began to wonder if the master storyteller was not mythic. Then one evening in Carrefour-Dufort two villagers rushed up to me and whispered: "Delaba has just returned from Port-au-Prince." (For weeks I had heard that Delaba, a goatherd,

5

was also a great *maître conte*.) "Where is he?" I whispered. "He's coming," they announced.

When Delaba arrived, the whole atmosphere changed. A group of teen-agers, children, and adults surrounded him, laughing and talking animatedly. He was tall, dark in color, and he had a charismatic presence. The storyteller who was speaking quickly finished, for all attention was on Delaba.

Delaba nodded to me, walked to the place the other storyteller had occupied, and began: "*Cric?*"

"*Crac!*" the others responded.

Delaba shook his head in disgust. He raised his voice: "*Cric?*"

And this time a resounding "*CRAC!*" answered him.

He smiled at his audience, pleased. It was this contact with his audience that differentiated Delaba from the other storytellers. Delaba not only created his own story, but he also played with the audience. If they sang loudly, he would raise his hand and admonish them. "Sweetly," he would say, or at other points in the story, "More, louder, stronger." And the audience complied.

He was an excellent entertainer. He varied his voice from contralto to falsetto, from loud to soft. He impersonated animals with gesture and voice. He sang and danced. When he danced, he not only turned in a circle clapping (as did Edouard, the narrator of "Bouki Dances the Kokioko"), but he

Photo by Odette Menesson Rigaud
Storytelling at Masson, Haiti. Storytellers and author.

also invented steps and gestures. He danced slowly, he danced fast. The audience loved him. They sang louder and louder. Again he admonished them, this time with a twinkle in his eye and a tilt of his head.

After each storytelling event, I would return with the *cric* on my Sony battery tape recorder. But the words of the story were not enough, for what was told and how and why was often affected by the *crac*, by the presence and reactions of the audience. By my second trip to Haiti, I began to take notes, either during the stories or after I had returned to my hotel.

Yet, when I began to compare the notes concerning the different storytellers with the quality of the stories that were told, I was surprised to find that there was often very little correspondence. Although Delaba was the best entertainer, none of his stories appear in this collection. The words of his stories did not have sufficient substance, beauty, or humor. And while Edouard was among the worst performers—his speech was often inaudible and garbled, his movements awkward—his story "Bouki Dances the Kokioko" is included. In a printed collection, words alone had to determine which of the storytellers' stories would be included. Yet who can measure the joy and delight that Delaba gave to others?

I thought about the brothers Grimm, Joseph Jacobs, and Harold Courlander, and about all the stories they had *not* included in their collections. I began to realize that story collectors, unlike folklorists, who make statistical samplings of all the stories they have gathered, choose in the end those stories they believe in.

Stories about the trickster team, Bouki and Malice, abound in Haiti. The history of Haiti has long been one of oppression, deprivation, and suffering. Twenty-five years after Columbus landed in Haiti, only a handful of the native Indian population remained. The Spanish brought slaves from Africa to work their sugar-cane and cotton plantations. When the French took control of the western part of the island in 1697, they continued to import slaves. Although Haiti has been independently governed since 1804, the majority of the people today still do not have enough to eat. Farmers are taxed on their produce to and from market. Infractions of governmental regulations are met with by severe punishments. People fix evil spells on their relatives and neighbors. This harsh reality of Haitian survival is reflected in a multitude of stories dealing with beatings, killings, shame, and dishonor. Clever little Malice triumphs; and big, stupid Bouki is fooled once again.

And the difficulties continue. In the 1970s, two thousand people inhabit each square mile of tillable soil, and over eighty-five percent of the populace cannot read or write. Education became free in

1816, but for more than a century only the rich could afford to pay for the supplies and books needed for schooling. The supplies have been free since 1946, but half the teachers have had no formal training and the books are in French. Since the peasant children grow up speaking Creole, which sounds similar to French but is structurally a different language, the illiteracy rate has not changed significantly. The farmers continue to be tied to the land, and the land is eroded and insufficient to provide for the children.

Yet, despite the inconsistencies, irrationalities, and intense problems of survival there *is* an order, a sense of life, and a richness of understanding among the Haitian peasants that goes beyond the daily poverty and difficulties and emerges in certain of their songs, proverbs, and stories.

In almost every story in this collection the background of hunger and survival exists, but there is also the humor ("I'm Tipingee, She's Tipingee, We're Tipingee, Too"), the silliness ("Cat Baptism"), the psychological insight ("The One Who Wouldn't Listen to His Own Dream"), the political acumen ("Horse and Toad"), the poetic imagery ("Papa God Sends Turtle Doves"), the wisdom ("The Forbidden Apple"), and the will to live ("The Magic Orange Tree") of a people who have not only survived but have done so with a creativity in art, song, dance, and story to rival Papa God.

If there is an abundance of stories with songs, *contes chantés*, that is because I am a storyteller and delighted in the participation of the audience in the story and with the storyteller. This enthusiastic communal participation is undoubtedly related to the religious experience of the people. The Voodoo priest or priestess does not speak to a passive, subdued congregation. On the contrary, it is the beat of the drum that announces the entrance of the spirits, and any member (regardless of age, status, or sex) of the singing, dancing congregation who is sufficiently immersed in the ceremony may be chosen by the spirits and possessed.

It is my hope that when you, my reader, turn the page and bite into the strange fruit of the Haitian night, your present world will dissolve and you will for the moment be possessed by the mysterious world of the spirit: the story.

Cric?

DIANE WOLKSTEIN

The Magic
Orange Tree

The Magic
Orange Tree

About the Story: When a child is born in the countryside, the umbilical cord may be saved and dried and planted in the earth, with a pit from a fruit tree placed on top of the cord. The tree that grows then belongs to the child. And when the tree gives fruit in five or six years, that fruit is considered the property of the child, who can barter or sell it. (Young children in Haiti very quickly become economically active.) Trees in Haiti are thus thought to protect children and are sometimes referred to as the guardian angel of the child. However, if the tree should die or grow in a deformed manner, that would be considered an evil omen for the child who owned the tree.

The song of the orange tree is often sung by the storyteller after the *cric?*, before the beginning of the story. Each storyteller may offer a slightly different melodic version of the song. Therefore, the storyteller's decision to sing before the story not only teaches the audience the storyteller's specific melody but also warms up the audience, for singing gets the blood flowing and the heart's juices jumping.

CRIC? CRAC!
There was once a girl whose mother died when she was born. Her father waited for some time to remarry, but when he did, he married a woman who was both mean and cruel. She was so mean there were some days she would not give the girl anything at all to eat. The girl was often hungry.

One day the girl came from school and saw on the table three round ripe oranges. *Hmmmm.* They smelled good. The girl looked around her. No one was there. She took one orange, peeled it, and ate it. *Hmmm-mmm.* It was good. She took a second orange and ate it. She ate the third orange. Oh-oh, she was happy. But soon her stepmother came home.

"Who has taken the oranges I left on the table?" she said. "Whoever has done so had better say their prayers now, for they will not be able to say them later."

The girl was so frightened she ran from the house. She ran through the woods until she came to her own mother's grave. All night she cried and prayed to her mother to help her. Finally she fell asleep.

In the morning the sun woke her, and as she rose to her feet something dropped from her skirit onto the ground. What was it? It was an orange pit. And the moment it entered the earth a green leaf sprouted from it. The girl watched, amazed. She knelt down and sang:*

> Orange tree,
> Grow and grow and grow.
> Orange tree, orange tree.
> Grow and grow and grow,
> Orange tree.
> Stepmother is not real mother,
> Orange tree.

The orange tree grew. It grew to the size of the girl. The girl sang:

* See music p. 196–197.

15

> Orange tree,
> Branch and branch and branch.
> Orange tree, orange tree,
> Branch and branch and branch,
> Orange tree.
> Stepmother is not real mother,
> Orange tree.

And many twisting, turning, curving branches appeared on the tree. Then the girl sang:

> Orange tree,
> Flower and flower and flower.
> Orange tree, orange tree,
> Flower and flower and flower,
> Orange tree.
> Stepmother is not real mother,
> Orange tree.

Beautiful white blossoms covered the tree. After a time they began to fade, and small green buds appeared where the flowers had been. The girl sang:

> Orange tree,
> Ripen and ripen and ripen.
> Orange tree, orange tree,
> Ripen and ripen and ripen,
> Orange tree.
> Stepmother is not real mother.
> Orange tree.

The oranges ripened, and the whole tree was filled with golden oranges. The girl was so delighted she danced around and around the tree, singing:

> Orange tree,
> Grow and grow and grow.

Orange tree, orange tree,
Grow and grow and grow,
Orange tree.
Stepmother is not real mother,
Orange tree.

But then when she looked, she saw the orange tree had grown up to the sky, far beyond her reach. What was she to do? Oh she was a clever girl. She sang:

Orange tree,
Lower and lower and lower.
Orange tree, orange tree,
Lower and lower and lower,
Orange tree.
Stepmother is not real mother,
Orange tree.

When the orange tree came down to her height, she filled her arms with oranges and returned home.

The moment the stepmother saw the gold oranges in the girl's arms, she seized them and began to eat them. Soon she had finished them all.

"Tell me, my sweet," she said to the girl, "where have you found such delicious oranges?"

The girl hesitated. She did not want to tell. The stepmother seized the girl's wrist and began to twist it.

"Tell me!" she ordered.

The girl led her stepmother through the woods to the orange tree. You remember the girl was very clever? Well, as soon as the girl came to the tree, she sang:

Orange tree,
Grow and grow and grow.
Orange tree, orange tree,
Grow and grow and grow,

Orange tree.
Stepmother is not real mother,
Orange tree.

And the orange tree grew up to the sky. What was the stepmother to do then? She began to plead and beg.

"Please," she said. "You shall be my own dear child. You may always have as much as you want to eat. Tell the tree to come down and
you shall pick the oranges for me." So the girl quietly sang:

Orange tree,
Lower and lower and lower.
Orange tree, orange tree,
Lower and lower and lower,
Orange tree.
Stepmother is not real mother,
Orange tree.

The tree began to lower. When it came to the height of the stepmother, she leapt on it and began to climb so quickly you might have
thought she was the daughter of an ape. And as she climbed from
branch to branch, she ate every orange. The girl saw that there would
soon be no oranges left. What would happen to her then? The girl
sang:

Orange tree,
Grow and grow and grow.
Orange tree, orange tree,
Grow and grow and grow,
Orange tree.
Stepmother is not real mother,
Orange tree.

The orange tree grew and grew and grew and grew. "Help!"
cried the stepmother as she rose into the sky. "H-E-E-lp. . . ."
The girl cried: *Break!* Orange tree, *Break!*

The orange tree broke into a thousand pieces . . . and the stepmother as well.

Then the girl searched among the branches until she found . . . a tiny orange pit. She carefully planted it in the earth. Softly she sang:

> Orange tree,
> Grow and grow and grow.
> Orange tree, orange tree,
> Grow and grow and grow,
> Orange tree.
> Stepmother is not real mother,
> Orange tree.

The orange tree grew to the height of the girl. She picked some oranges and took them to market to sell. They were so sweet the people bought all her oranges.

Every Saturday she is at the marketplace selling her oranges. Last Saturday, I went to see her and asked her if she would give me a free orange. "What?" she cried. "After all I've been through!" And she gave me such a kick in the pants that that's how I got here today, to tell you the story—"The Magic Orange Tree."

The Two Donkeys

The Two Donkeys

About the Story: When Willy and I first arrived in Carrefour-Dufort, I was a great curiosity. Within minutes of getting out of the car, a crowd of all ages surrounded me. Willy, who had once lived in the village as an assistant to an anthropology student, saw an old girlfriend and disappeared.

Several years before, when I was working for the parks department in New York City, telling stories to children in Harlem and Bedford-Stuyvesant, I had also from time to time found myself the only white person among a large crowd of black people. Then, the people had immediately asked me who I was and why I had come. Now, no one was speaking; they were staring and pointing and whispering.

I noticed one little girl smiling shyly at me. I bent down and smiled at her. At once her hand darted out. Quickly she touched my hair. (It is blond and fairly straight.) Even more quickly she brought her hand back close to her side. Everyone laughed.

"*Bonsoir, messieurs-dames,*" I said. A great singsong response echoed: "*Bonjour, mademoiselle.*" "No," someone said, "she's married, she's wearing a ring." I pointed to my ring and nodded and at once the questions began in Creole:

"Do you have children?" "Yes."

"How many?" "One. A girl."

"What's her name?" "Rachel."

"Where is she?" "In Port-au-Prince."

"Where is your husband?" "In New York."

"What's his name?" "Benjamin."

"What's your name?" "Diane"

"How old are you?" "Thirty-one." (Great consternation!)

"Why don't you have more children?"

That was enough.

"What's your name?" I asked a young woman near me. Complete silence. I hadn't followed the proper order of questioning. I waited. We looked at each other. I waited. It was almost dusk and the odor of the night blew up from the river. "My name is Justine," a dark, pretty girl offered. At that moment Willy reappeared.

He explained that I told stories and wanted to hear stories and would pay a small sum of money for a good story. Immediately there were shouts: "I'll tell a story." "I'll give a story." "I have one."

"Silence!" Willy shouted. "Where shall we go?" he asked. "My house," Dadi offered. With that, about thirty children and adults trooped off to Dadi's house.

We didn't go inside. The houses are not more than ten feet by fifteen feet. In the clearing in front of the house the storytelling began. I took out my notebook and pen, switched on my tape recorder, and listened.

Although my own Creole was halting, I could usually follow the general movement of the plot. But sometimes, especially when the storyteller did not speak clearly, I was lost. I listened instead to the frogs croaking and to the crickets. The Haitian night was very dark and voluptuous.

But when Julien began "The Two Donkeys," my attention was immediately caught. His gruff voice described the love of the donkeys and his quite masculine body swayed to and fro in the most feminine manner, imitating sensual passion. The others were equally caught by Julien's antics as he changed his voice and body for the enraptured farmer, the angry farmer, the "good" farmer's wife, and the ecstatic donkeys. The most wonderful moment of the pantomime came when Julien pulled back the seat of his pants to show us how the woman's skirt had been pushed out by the growth of her tail. When Julien got to the part where the husband returned home, the audience was so excited one woman beat him to the punchline by calling out: "Didn't she break every pot and plate in the house?" "Yes," Julien reassured her, "*every* pot and plate." "Good! Good!" she shouted. Julien delivered his last lines to the accompaniment of great applause and laughter.

THERE were once two donkeys who were always together. A male donkey and a female donkey. They ate grass on the mountainside, rubbing each other's long necks with their heads. They rolled on the grass, playfully biting each other's ears, frolicking and frisking.

Then one year there was a dry season. The worst that anyone had ever known. No rain fell. No plants grew, no shrubs, not even one blade of grass.

"We shall both die if this continues," the male donkey said to his wife. "I have a plan. Let us change ourselves into human beings. I shall become a man and find work with whoever can pay me. You change into a woman and stay wherever you can find work. Then when the rainy season comes again, we shall both change back into donkeys and meet here as we were before."

The female donkey agreed. She changed into a woman and was so beautiful that she was married that evening to a farmer who saw her, fell in love with her, and couldn't wait. The male donkey changed into a man and also found a place to stay. And the dry season passed.

Six months went by. The rains began and moistened the ground. The faded earth was soon filled with life and covered with flowers and grass. The man changed back into a donkey and ran eagerly to the mountain, but his wife was not there. He waited, and when she did not return, he began to travel from town to town, calling her:

Anne, Anne*

for that was his wife's name.

Anne, Anne,
Springtime has come again
Anne—

At last one day he came to the town where Anne was living. She was in the kitchen peeling malengas and yams for her husband's dinner.

Anne, Anne,

She dropped the yams and listened.

Springtime has come again
Anne, Anne—

Her ears became longer, her two arms began stretching, and from under her skirt a tail started pushing.

The farmer, waiting in the fields for his dinner, was getting angry. "I told my wife to bring my dinner by noon. And where is she? What can she be doing at the house all this time?"

As the farmer came near his home, ready to give his wife a good beating, he heard a great crash as if a pot had been broken. *Pow!* Then out the kitchen door trotted a female donkey. *HEE-huh HEE-huh.*

* If you pronounce Anne as Ahnne, you will join in on the Creole-French pun in which Ahnne (*âne*) also means donkey.

A male donkey who was waiting by the gate rushed up to her and they both stood on their hind legs, braying with pleasure and biting each other's long ears. *HEE-huh! HEE-huh! HEE-huh!* Then they turned toward the hills and ran happily out of town to the mountains.

The man went into the kitchen and found his wife was gone, and every pot and plate in the kitchen was broken. Every pot and plate. Everything!

Well, I tell you this story because I want to point out to you how important it is to have a proper engagement, and how necessary it is to meet your future bride or bridegroom's relatives—the sisters, brothers, aunts, uncles, cousins, and especially the mother. Otherwise, if you are too hasty, such a thing can happen. It can. And to you.

Owl

Owl

About the Story: This storytelling was the most exciting I have ever witnessed. It took place at Masson, a sugar-cane area about ten miles from Port-au-Prince. The storyteller, Rosemarie Masse, was fifty years old. She was thin and muscular. She stood erect and proud in her faded, blue dress. As she began, she chose a teen-age girl to help her. That particular girl was a good choice, for she had a loud, strong, infectious voice and was proud to be in the center of the gathering.

At the point in the story where Owl arrives at the girl's house, Rosemarie ran to one of the men on the outskirts of the crowd and grabbed his straw hat. She set it on her own head at a becoming tilt. Everyone laughed. Then, when the dance began, "Dong ga da, Dong," Rosemarie clapped her hands and nodded to her young partner. The partner then took over the singing, and Rosemarie began to dance.

She danced holding herself perfectly erect, moving only her hips and chest, with her arms outspread. She danced with such beauty and grace and sexuality, I wanted to join, but I wanted even more to watch her. The young children immediately began to dance in place; everyone else was clapping and singing. Each time Rosemarie danced, the sing-

ing and clapping must have lasted from five to fifteen minutes. Her young partner's voice maintained
its strength and power, and the audience of about
fifty people gave Rosemarie their full support.

I whispered to one of the villagers that Rosemarie danced well. "Of course," he replied. "It is
the old women who know how to dance. They
have lived."

OWL thought he was very ugly. But one
evening he met a girl and talked with
her and she liked him. "If it had been day," Owl thought, "and she had
seen my face, she never would have liked me." But still she had liked
him.

So Owl went to her house the next night. And the next. And the
night after that. Every evening he would arrive at the girl's house at
seven, and they would sit outside on the porch steps, talking together
politely.

Then one evening after Owl had left, the girl's mother said to
her, "Why doesn't your fiancé come and visit you during the day?"

"But Mama, he's explained that to me. He works during the day.
Then he must go home and change and he cannot get here before
seven."

"Still, I would like to see his face before the marriage," the mother
said. "Let's invite him to our house for a dance this Sunday afternoon.
Surely he doesn't work on Sunday."

Owl was very pleased with the invitation: a dance in his honor.
But he was also very frightened. He told his cousin, Rooster, about
the girl and asked him to accompany him to the dance. But that Sunday afternoon, as Owl and Rooster were riding on their horses to the
dance, Owl glanced over at Rooster. Rooster held himself with such
assurance, he was so elegantly and fashionably dressed, that Owl
imagined the girl seeing the two of them and was filled with shame.

"I can't go on," he choked. "You go and tell them I've had an
accident and will be there later."

Rooster rode to the dance. "Tsk tsk, poor Owl," he explained. "He has had an accident, and he has asked me to let you know that he will be here later."

When it was quite dark, Owl tied his horse a good distance from the dance and stumbled up to the porch steps.

"Pssst," he whispered to a young man sitting on the steps. "Is Rooster here?"

"Well now, I don't know."

"Go and look. Tell him a friend is waiting for him by the mapou* tree."

Rooster came out. "OWL!"

"Shhhhhh—"

"*Owl!*"

"Shhh—"

"Owl, what are you wearing over your head—I mean your face?"

"It's a hat. Haven't you ever seen a hat before? Look, tell them anything. Tell them I scratched my eyes on a branch as I was riding here and the light—even the light from a lamp—hurts them. And you must be certain to watch for the day for me, and to crow as soon as you see the light, so we can leave."

"Yes, yes," Rooster said. "Come in and I shall introduce you to the girl's relatives."

Rooster introduced Owl to everyone, explaining Owl's predicament. Owl went around shaking hands, his hat hung down almost completely covering his face. Owl then tried to retreat into a corner, but the girl came over.

"Come into the yard and let's dance,*" she said.

> Dong ga da, Dong ga da, Dong ga da, Dong.
> Dong ga da, Dong. Eh-ee-oh.

Owl danced. And Owl could dance well. The girl was proud of Owl. Even if he wore his hat strangely and had sensitive eyes, he *could* dance.

* *mapou* (pronounced ma-pu) is believed in Haiti to be inhabited by evil spirits.
* See music p. 197.

Dong ga da, Dong ga da, Dong ga da, Dong.
Dong ga da, Dong. Eh-ee-oh.

Rooster was dancing too. When Owl noticed that Rooster was dancing, instead of watching for the day, Owl was afraid that Rooster would forget to warn him, and he excused himself to the girl. He ran out of the yard, past the houses to a clearing where he could see the horizon. No, it was still night. Owl came back.

Dong ga da, Dong ga da, Dong ga da, Dong.
Dong ga da, Dong. Eh-ee-oh.

Owl motioned to Rooster, but Rooster was lost in the dance. Owl excused himself again to the girl, ran to the clearing; no, it was still night. Owl returned.

Dong ga da, Dong ga da, Dong ga da, Dong.
Dong ga da, Dong. Eh-ee-oh.

Owl tried to excuse himself again, but the girl held on to him. "Yes, stay with me," she said. And so they danced and danced and danced.

Dong ga da, Dong ga da, Dong ga da, Dong.
Dong ga da, Dong. Eh-ee-oh.

The sun moved up in the sky, higher and higher, until it filled the house and the yard with light.

"Now—let us see your fiancé's face!" the mother said.

"*Kokioko!*"* Rooster crowed.

And before Owl could hide, she reached out and pulled the hat from his face.

"MY EYES!" Owl cried, and covering his face with his hands, he ran for his horse.

"Wait, Owl!" the girl called.

* Kokioko-(Ko-kee-o-ko), is Creole for cock-a-doodle-doo.

"*Kokioko!*" Rooster crowed.

"Wait, Owl, wait."

And as Owl put his hands down to untie his horse, the girl saw his face. It was striking and fierce, and the girl thought it was the most handsome face she had ever seen.

"Owl—"

But Owl was already on his horse, riding away, farther and farther away.

Owl never came back.

The girl waited. Then she married Rooster. She was happy, except sometimes in the morning when Rooster would crow "kokioko-o-o." Then she would think about Owl and wonder where he was.

Put That
Man to Bed

Put That
Man to Bed

About the Story: Sexual matters are discussed freely
by Haitian peasants before their children. The
woman is proud of her sexuality, the man of his
virility. It is said of a young girl who has not had
a relationship with a man: "She does not know
life." The Haitian peasant mother believes that by
the time her daughter is eighteen, she should find a
husband and eventually have children.

For this reason Chofi's mother tells Chofi to invite the young man into the house. She knows that
the man is a possible husband. He is the one who
frees her from the snake, allowing her access to the
"waters of life." The mother also understands that
young girls, not always knowing quite what a man
wants, need encouragement.

Chofi's story was told on the porch of Jeanne
Philippe's house in Thor. Thor is on the way south
to Jacmel, about a twenty-minute drive from Port-
au-Prince. Gathered on Dr. Philippe's porch were
seven storytellers, Jeanne, her parents, and about
fifteen children from the neighborhood, who appeared as soon as the first storyteller began.

Solange Cidé, the storyteller, might herself
have been Chofi. Eighteen years old, very pretty,
and newly arrived from Jacmel, Solange spoke with

great shyness and with frequent blushing. The audience loved the story. Each time the mother screamed, gales of laughter came from the listeners. Even though Solange told the tale in a quiet, reserved manner, the story itself brought forth a vociferous response, as do most stories in Haiti that center around sex.

ONE day Chofi's* mother sent her to the spring to bring back water. But when Chofi came near the spring, a snake, who was lying by the edge of the spring, uncoiled itself and hissed at her.

Chofi drew back and waited. She waited until she thought the snake had gone back to sleep. Then she quietly approached the spring. But the snake arose immediately and again hissed at her. Chofi waited.

She waited a long time, but each time she thought the snake had gone to sleep, it would uncurl itself and hiss at her.

At last Chofi saw a man walking in the woods near by. She ran to him and asked him if he could kill the snake for her.

"Of course," said the man. "But what will you give me in return?"

"I will pay you," said Chofi.

"I don't need money."

"I will give you food."

"I am not hungry."

"Then I will give you something else," said Chofi.

The man agreed and killed the snake for Chofi.

When Chofi returned home with her calabash filled with water, she did not tell her mother what had happened. The two ate dinner and went to sleep.

At ten o'clock the mother woke up. Someone was singing outside the gate:

* Chofi is pronounced "Shófee." The girl's name is a pun on the Creole-French word *chauffer*, to warm up.

> Chofi, Chofi
> I killed the snake for you
> And cut my foot.
>
> You promised me money
> I told you no.
> You promised me food
> I told you no.
>
> Chofi, Chofi,
> Give me what you promised.

The mother called to Chofi: "Someone is at the gate asking for you."

"Mama, I am not expecting anyone."

But the man continued singing:

> Chofi, Chofi
> I killed the snake for you
> And cut my foot.

"Chofi," said the mother. "Get up this minute and let the man inside."

Chofi went to the gate, and the man followed her up the path.

"Stay here on the porch," Chofi said. And she went back to sleep. But the man did not like sitting there alone, so he began to sing again:

> Chofi, Chofi

"Chofi," her mother shouted. "This man will wake up all the neighbors. Bring him inside the house."

Chofi did as her mother told her.

The man waited a long time, but as Chofi did not return, the man started to cry like a baby, "Chofiiii, Chofiiii." Then he was singing and crying at the same time:

You promised me money
I told you no.
You promised me food
I told you no.

"THUNDER AND LIGHTNING!"* Chofi's mother screamed. "What does this man want? Chofi, bring him into your bedroom and tell him to go to sleep."

Chofi went to the man and led him into her room. "Sit down there," she said to him, pointing to the far corner of the room.

The man sat down and immediately began singing:

Chofi, Chofi

"Chofi!" cried her mother. "*Put that man to bed.*"

So Chofi led him to the bed and told him to lie down at one end. "Be quiet now," she said to him, and she lay down at the other end.

For a time the man did not sing. He seemed to be happy. But when Chofi turned her back on him and went to sleep, he began to sing and cry all over again:

Chofi, Chofi
I killed the snake for you
And cut my foot.

"Chofi," shouted her mother, "this is the third time I've told you: put that man to bed."

"But he is in bed, Mama."

"Then cover him up. He must be cold."

So Chofi gave him part of the sheet. But the man was still not happy and continued singing:

Chofi, Chofi

* A free translation from the Creole epithet, Tonnerre.

"Chofi," shouted the mother. "Warm that man up!"

When the man heard that, he slid over to Chofi's side and embraced her. Soon Chofi turned out the light, and the man did not sing again.

Four Hairs
from the Beard
of the Devil

Four Hairs
from the Beard
of the Devil

About the Story: Oh-oh is a Haitian exclamation
expressing surprise, approval, trouble, delight, and
many other feelings. The two words are almost
sung, at a pitch about a fifth above the storyteller's
normal speaking voice, and both "ohs" are voiced on
the same tone. I've rarely heard a Haitian story
without at least one oh-oh, but Julien's oh-ohs were
small dramas in themselves.

When kings appear in Haitian folktales they
are frequently ridiculed. In point of fact, kings
were not a part of Haitian history but power sym-
bols coming from the royal tradition in African
and European folktales. With one "oh-oh," Julien
suggested the pride, bearing, stupidity, and greed of
"the Ruler," in this case King John.

Julien, the raconteur of "The Two Donkeys,"
was a moody, spontaneous, and witty storyteller.
He told "Four Hairs from the Beard of the Devil"
on a friend's porch in Carrefour-Dufort to a group
of fellow farmers, most of whom were also in their
early twenties. He had a natural way of using an-
cient expressions, such as, "honor" and "respect,"
and an equal facility for throwing in comments to
please his contemporaries: "All kings are fools."

Julien usually dramatized the physical descrip-
tions in his stories—limping when a limp is men-

tioned, miming the removal of a hair from his beardless chin, jumping up from the shock of his own loud snoring. But at other times, when there was little drama in a story, Julien's voice would become heavy, coated, and tired. He would speak as if he were about to fall asleep. Then suddenly, he would unravel the rest of the story in one breath, shout *"Cric?,"* and gallop off into the next story with the excitement of a young boy who has been given just the toy he's always wanted.

T HERE was once a young boy who lived with his stepmother, and she didn't like him at all. She was always giving him difficult tasks to do, but whatever she asked, he always did.

Then one day, she thought of a way to get rid of him. She made a small cotton sack and said to him, "I want you to bring me back four hairs from the beard of the devil in this sack."

Now the boy didn't know how he would be able to pull four hairs from the devil's beard, nor did he even know where the devil lived, but he was not afraid. He took the sack and set out down the road.

He came upon the king of Spain walking in the woods with his daughter, who was limping badly.

"Young boy," asked the king, "where are you going whistling like that?"

"Honor,* I am on a mission to bring back four hairs from the beard of the devil for my stepmother."

"Oh-oh! Well, if you ever get there, and I doubt very much you will," said the king, "but if you do, would you ask the devil what I can do for my daughter's sore foot? For three years she's been limping like this. Show him, child."

---

* "Honor" is an old form of respect offered to elders and to those in a superior social position. In the mountains a person who is approaching will call out "Honor," and the one addressed will answer "Respect" to let the newcomer know he is welcomed.

The girl limped a little in front of them, and the boy shook his head sadly.

"I will surely ask the devil," he said.

A day later the boy met another king, King John.

"Where are you off to, young lad?" King John asked.

"Honor, to the house of the devil, to bring back four hairs from his beard to my stepmother."

"Oh-oh. Well, my boy, if they don't eat you when you get there, would you ask the devil why my well has been dry for two months now?"

"I will, honor," the boy said and walked on.

"Halt!" a guard called out, pointing his gun at the boy. "Where are you going?"

"I am on my way to the house of the devil to bring back four hairs from his beard to my stepmother."

"To the big devil?" the guard said in awe.

"That's right."

"Come over here," the guard whispered. "Please, would you speak to him for me? I have been standing here for three years now, holding this gun, and no one has come to relieve me. I do not know what to do. Ask him what I should do, and if you get a good answer I'll give you half of what I own."

"All right," the boy said, and he continued walking and walking until he came to a house that looked like the house where the devil might live. He knocked on the door and the devil's wife came to answer it.

"Honor," he said politely and bowed.

Now the devil's wife appreciated being addressed in such a polite manner.

"Respect," she answered. "Come in, little boy." And when she looked at the boy she liked him and didn't want the devil to eat him.

"What did you come for?" she asked.

And the boy told her what his stepmother wanted, what the king of Spain wanted, what King John wanted, and what the guard wanted.

"Not so difficult," she said, "if you can stay awake the night. Now run and hide under the bed."

"I SMELL FRESH MEAT!" the devil shouted as he entered the house.

"Of course you do, my dear," said his wife. "It is your dinner waiting for you on the table. Let us sit down and eat."

After they had eaten, they went to bed, and as soon as the devil began to snore, zzzZZzzz, his wife reached over and took one of the hairs of his beard and began to twist it. She twisted and twisted it. *Fsst.* She pulled it out.

Then she took a second hair and began to twist it. *Fsssst.* It was out. Oh. The devil woke up.

"Who is pulling my beard?" he asked.

"Oh-oh, did I do that?" said the wife sleepily. "I must have been dreaming."

"What was your dream?" the devil asked.

"The king of Spain is walking in the woods with his daughter. She is limping. He is so sad. He does not know how to help her—"

"What a fool! All he needs to do is to crush the sulfur rock in front of his house and put the powder on his daughter's toe and the sore will disappear. . . . Kings are fools. Wife, go to sleep."

"Yes, yes," she said.

She waited and when her husband was snoring again, zzzzZZ, she took a third hair and began to twist it. *Fsst.* It was out.

"Ooh. Are you pulling my beard again?"

"Oh? Did I do that again? I was dreaming another dream."

"Tell me your dream."

"King John is sitting near his well. He is thirsty, but there is no water to drink. The well is dry."

"Number-two fool! Let him take out the guava that is plugging up the bottom of his well and his well will be filled with water. All kings are fools."

"You are right," his wife agreed. "I will go back to sleep."

For the last time, the devil's wife reached over, took a hair from his beard, and began to twist it. *Fssst.* The fourth hair was out.

"Wife, what is it now?"

"I just had another dream. What a night I am having."

"Tell me this dream," the devil said.

47

"A guard is standing at attention, pointing his gun. He has been standing there for three years now. No one has come to relieve him—"

"The biggest of fools!" cried the devil. "Let him stop the first man who passes and ask the man to hold his gun while he buys a pack of cigarettes and that's that."

"That's that," the wife said, and went to sleep.

"That's that," the boy added from under the bed.

Before dawn, the woman woke up. She gave the boy the four hairs from the devil's beard and wished him luck. He thanked her and set out on his way.

The boy waved his sack with the four frizzled hairs at the guard.

"Did you really see the great devil?" the guard asked.

"Honor, I did. And I have an answer for you. Just ask the first person who passes to hold your gun, say you have to buy a pack of cigarettes, say anything—then you'll be free."

"How simple," the guard said. And he took all his money out of his knapsack. As he was handing the boy the last penny, he said, "Excuse me, could you hold this—"

"Not *me!*" the boy said. "Ask the next person who passes. Good luck!"

"Halt!" the guard cried, for someone was already passing. The boy kept walking as a young man took the gun from the guard.

The boy advised King John to remove the guava that was blocking his well, and soon water was gushing up its sides. King John rewarded the boy with a donkey loaded with two sacks of gold.

The boy continued on his way and pointed out the sulfur rock to the king of Spain. The king of Spain thanked him and asked the boy to come back for his money. Then the boy went home.

"Honor, here is your sack and inside are the four hairs from the beard of the devil." The stepmother could not believe it. As she examined the four grizzly hairs, the boy looked around for the last time, then he said, "I must go now, for someone still owes me money."

The king of Spain's daughter was now cured and was walking, skipping and running. The boy was well paid, but he did not return home with his money, nor did he go anywhere else. He was perfectly content at the house of the king of Spain.

The Case
of the
Uncooked Eggs

The Case
of the
Uncooked Eggs

About the Story: Dadi, a peasant woman in her
forties, told this story the same evening Julien told
"The Two Donkeys." I heard Dadi tell many stories
and never tired of watching her. She spoke with
assurance and composure in a high, clear nasal
voice. She had prominent cheekbones and a soft,
proud face. Although people would afterward tell
me that they knew Dadi's stories, she had such a
captivating effect on everyone that her audiences of
children and adults would listen as if they had
never heard the story before.

As Dadi began the story a neighbor punc-
tuated each business transaction with "yes . . . yes."
He seemed to be both reinforcing the validity of
the story and supporting Dadi's storytelling. But as
soon as the woman in the story received the summons to go to court, the neighbor was quiet, as was
everyone else.

The account Dadi gives of raising animals and
buying land describes accurately the ambitions of
almost every Haitian peasant. No matter how much
land a child is given, there is never enough. If a
child inherits land from his parents, he is considered
fortunate; but if a person has been able to purchase
land by his own work and accomplishment, that
person is considered "a success."

Once, in the marketplace in Kenscoff, a man was pointed out to me as being very rich. He was reputed to own hundreds of acres of land. "How can that be?" I asked. "He looks like a peasant." I was assured that he was very wise to dress that way (in a plain cotton shirt, pants, and a new straw hat); otherwise, he might attract the evil eye.

This may have been what happened to Dadi's heroine when she all too graciously revealed the full extent of her "success."

A poor woman in Kenscoff once offered lodging to a soldier, and before he left he gave her a gift of three eggs. She looked at the eggs. They were longer on one end. She decided not to cook them but to put them under the hen to hatch.

Soon three fat red roosters peeped out of the shells. The woman raised the roosters and took them to market and sold them for five dollars. With the money, she bought two small pigs. She nourished the pigs on banana peels and corn and sold them for a goat. She sold the goat for a calf, and when the calf had grown into a strong ox, she sold it and bought land.

Some years later, the same soldier was again passing through Kenscoff and asked for lodging at the woman's house.

"Oh, don't you recognize me?" she cried. "When you were here last you gave me three eggs. I never forget when someone does me a good turn."

She was so happy to see him she made him a large meal, and as they ate together, she told him what she had done with the three eggs. After they had finished their coffee, she took him around her property and showed him her fields of carrots, tomatoes, leeks, and radishes; her cattle; even her flowers. He stayed with her for five days. She treated him royally and then he left.

Eight days later she received a summons to appear in court. As she had never done any harm to anyone in her life, she did not go. A week later, she received a second summons. She ignored this one as well. But when the third summons came, she woke at two in the morning and walked five hours to town.

Waiting for her in the courthouse was the soldier. He declared that because of his gift to her of three eggs, she was able to buy livestock, fields, and even roses and violets. Now it was only correct that she share her goods with him.

"But the soldier did not give me roosters," she told the judge, "he only gave me eggs!"

"Yes, and those eggs, did they not give you all that you have?" the soldier insisted.

The woman left the courthouse. She hired a lawyer. The soldier hired a lawyer. The case went on and on; the two lawyers deliberating endlessly. As the case came to a close the woman was so exhausted, she was nearly willing to divide her property with the soldier.

Then, on the Thursday evening before the final decision was to be made on Monday, an old ragged beggar knocked on her door.

"Charity for a poor man," he said. "A little something to eat."

"Not at this moment," she said. "I am not giving out charity. I do not even know what I will have tomorrow." And she explained the case to him.

"Madame, don't you worry; nothing serious will happen!"

"Nothing serious! It's almost all over!" But she relented and offered him some bread and rice and beans.

Then he said, "Madame, here is some advice. Eat well on Saturday and Sunday. Get up early Monday, make yourself coffee, walk to town, and I will be waiting for you in the court."

The woman looked at him. "*You* will be waiting for me. But what can you do?"

"You shall see."

Sunday, just before midnight, the woman woke up. She prepared coffee for herself and started down to Port-au-Prince. The beggar was already seated on one of the benches. The woman sat down. The lawyers arrived and the final speeches were made. They talked and talked and talked. The woman felt so tired she was certain that if someone

dropped a handkerchief on her, she would fall to the floor and not be able to get up.

Just then the old beggar called out: "Judge!"

"What is it, old vagabond?"

"I have come to hear the verdict."

"Why should an old beggar like you concern yourself with the verdict of this case?"

"Several days ago, this good woman gave me as charity some of her dinner of rice and beans. I ate the rice but brought the beans home to plant. I told my friend I have seven beans to plant and he offered me space in his fields. He is at this moment in the fields waiting for me. And now I am waiting for you, for your decision. I want to know whether it is worth the effort for me to plant my beans."

The people in the courthouse laughed and shouted. The lawyers stood up to look at the man.

The judge said, "Whoever heard of cooked beans being planted?"

"Thank you, judge," said the beggar. "When this good woman told me it was believed in court that eggs could provide flowers and pigs and goats, I thought, perhaps I, too, should make the effort. After all, if the laws have been changed, and eggs can give all that, what can beans do?"

Everyone shouted, "Bravo!"

The case was dismissed. The woman had won.

Tayzanne

Tayzanne

About the Story: Although most stories told in Haiti do not have titles, the more popular ones do have names. When a storyteller is about to tell a well-known tale, he will shout out its name after the *crac!* The two stories I heard called out the most often in Haiti were "Tayzanne" and "The Magic Orange Tree."

The first time I heard "The Magic Orange Tree," I loved it and knew at once that I would tell it. Then, to my delight, when I heard it a second time, there were even more details I wanted to add. Many times after that when listening to the story, a particular turn of phrase or joke or description struck me and I would add it to my original version.

It was different with "Tayzanne." Each time I heard it I would sing along with the others. But later, when I would think about the story itself, I could not quite grasp it. Only the song remained in my mind, the haunting poignant melody of *"Tézin, mon ami, moi, zin"* (see music on page 198–199). I would then listen again to the story on my tape recorder, but each version fell short of a certain fullness. I prepared the manuscript of Haitian stories, without "Tayzanne." And yet I kept asking myself, how can I offer a collection of Haitian stories without "Tayzanne"?

On my last trip to Haiti, I heard four more versions, not one that I liked, and I loved the song more and more. When I came back to New York, I checked all the versions to be certain I had not been too severe. But the words would not magically change themselves.

Then, one afternoon in New York, at the Art Foods Restaurant, I sat at a table with Chuck Mee, a friend and fellow writer, and found myself telling him about the elusive quality of Haitian stories.

He said, "What seems to me most mysterious is how you, the storyteller, received each story."

"But I haven't even told all the stories I heard. I can't even figure out how to put one of the most fantastic stories into the book."

"Tell me that one," he said.

"Okay," I said, lowering my voice, "I'm going to tell you 'Tayzanne.' " And there, in the clatter of the noonday dishes, I half whispered and half told "Tayzanne." "But that's marvelous," he said when I'd finished. "You *have* to put that one in the book. Tell it just that way."

Later, as I typed the story, I realized that the version I'd told him was a combination of versions I had heard from Solange at Thor, Justine at Carrefour-Dufort, and that of Suzanne-Comhaire Sylvain in *Contes Haitiens*. It had taken five years for the different versions of "Tayzanne" to knit themselves together, whereas I had eagerly told "The Magic Orange Tree" a week after hearing it. If there is a question about which Haitian story is most accessible, the answer probably depends on the receptivity of the translator. Even the most popular Haitian story must be "received" before it can be revealed.

EVERY day, either Velina or her younger brother went to the spring to bring back water. One morning, when Velina dipped her bucket into the water, her ring fell off. Ahh-hh. The waters stirred. Up came a great silver-golden fish.

"Have you seen my ring?" Velina asked.

The fish disappeared into the waters and came up again with Velina's ring on his nose.

"Oh, thank you," said the girl. "My name is Velina. I live nearby and come almost every day to the spring for water. But I did not know you lived here."

The fish said, "My name is Tayzanne.* I live in the deepest part of the spring. If you would like, I will take your bucket and bring you water that is cool and sweet."

Velina held out her bucket and the fish took it and disappeared under the spring. Down he went. Down and down. And then he appeared again with Velina's bucket filled with clear, sweet water. Velina thanked him and went home.

After some days, the girl's mother noticed that the water Velina brought back from the spring was always clearer than that which her brother brought back. She spoke to the little boy and told him to pay more attention to where he got his water. Several days later, she saw it was still muddy. She scolded the boy and said, "I told you to pay more attention when you dip your bucket into the water. I want you to bring back water as clear as your sister's."

So the little boy decided to follow Velina the next morning to see where she dipped her bucket into the water. He walked quietly behind Velina, and hid behind a tree, and watched as Velina came to the edge of the spring and sang:

* Tayzanne (pronounced—Tey-zahnne) is *Tézin* in Creole. In Creole *zin* means "hook" and *té* is the past tense. Literally, then, *Tézin* means "hooked," but the Creole song insists on *Tézin* being called *zin* as well. He is thus the hook *and* the hooked. In his dual role, Tayzanne the fish entices the young girl away from her family and toward the spirits.

Tayzanne, fish of the clear spring,
Tayzanne, fish of the deep.
Tayzanne, my friend,
My friend, Tayzanne, Tayzanne,
Tayzanne, my friend,
O come to me.

Then he went home and told his mother that the next day he could bring back water as clear as Velina's.

"How will you do it?" his mother asked.

"It will be easy. I will do as Velina. I will sing to the fish in the spring and when he comes out I will give him my bucket and he will give me clear, sweet water just as he does for Velina."

"No, no," said the mother. "You must not do that. That is an evil spirit who lives in the water. I will go myself."

That evening the mother followed Velina to the spring. She hid and listened as Velina sang:

Tayzanne, fish of the clear spring,
Tayzanne, fish of the deep.
Tayzanne, my friend,
My friend, Tayzanne, Tayzanne,
Tayzanne, my friend,
O come to me.

Then she saw the silver-golden fish leap from the waters and take Velina's bucket and return with it filled with water. She went home.

But Tayzanne, through his powers, understood the mother's intentions, and told Velina that her mother would try to kill him. He told her that if she saw three drops of blood on her breast she would know that her mother had succeeded. Velina started to cry when she heard this, but Tayzanne said she need not worry for in the end they would be together.

The mother told her husband that there was an evil spirit in the spring who was consorting with their daughter and that they must kill it the next day.

In the morning, Velina's mother sent her to market to sell vegetables. Velina did not want to go, but she had to obey. The mother and father and the little brother went to the spring. In a stern voice the mother sang:

> Tayzanne, fish of the clear spring,
> Tayzanne, fish of the deep.
> Tayzanne, my friend,
> My friend, Tayzanne, Tayzanne,
> Tayzanne, my friend,
> O come to me.

There was no movement in the waters. "You sing," she said to her son, "your voice is lighter. It is closer to Velina's." The boy sang softly:

> Tayzanne, fish of the clear spring,
> Tayzanne, fish of the deep.
> Tayzanne, my friend,
> My friend, Tayzanne, Tayzanne,
> Tayzanne, my friend,
> O come to me.

The fish leaped up. He was very large. The father threw the rope he had brought with him. He threw it like a lasso and caught the silver-golden fish. But the fish was so powerful it did not die. The father had to take out his machete to kill it.

Velina was sad all day. In the afternoon her breast felt damp. She thought it was her tears, but when she looked down at her white blouse she saw three drops of blood. Quickly she gathered together her vegetables and went home. She entered the house and saw her mother was cooking a large fish over the fire. She ran out. She ran to the spring. She sang:

> Tayzanne, fish of the clear spring,
> Tayzanne, fish of the deep.

> Tayzanne, my friend,
> My friend, Tayzanne, Tayzanne,
> Tayzanne, my friend,
> O come to me.

The waters were still. Velina went home. But she would not enter the house. She sat on a chair outside. She began to comb her hair. Looking into a small mirror and combing her hair, she sang and she wept:

> Tayzanne, fish of the clear spring,
> Tayzanne, fish of the deep.
> Tayzanne, my friend,
> My friend, Tayzanne, Tayzanne,
> Tayzanne, my friend,
> O come to me.

Her brother heard her singing and came out. Ah. What he saw. The chair she was sitting on was sinking into the earth.

"Velina! Velina, stop crying," he said. "Your tears are softening the earth."

But Velina was so filled with sadness she did not hear him.

The brother ran inside. "Papa, Papa, come quick. Velina is sinking into the earth."

"It is late," the father answered. "You are imagining things, go to bed."

"But Papa, please, please."

The brother ran outside again. Velina had sunk into the earth up to her waist.

"Mama, Mama, Mama," he cried, "you must come, Velina is sinking into the earth."

"Nonsense," said the mother, but the boy pleaded so desperately that she went outside just as Velina's shoulders sank into the earth. The mother ran and grabbed her daughter by the hair, but the rest of her had already been swallowed up. The mother stood there and the brother too, in the night—and all that was left was Velina's hair.

Cat and Dog
and the Return
of the Dead

Cat and Dog
and the Return
of the Dead

About the Story: When Dog says, "Everyone is forever mourning the dead," this is more than true in Haiti. The spirits that the people serve are their dead parents and distant ancestors. And the Haitian dead are extremely exigent, bringing illness and bad fortune to their children when they are displeased. Perhaps a living person did not serve sufficient food and drink at the wake, or erect a tombstone, or leave flowers or a candle at the grave. To find out which spirit is angry, and why, a *hungan* or *mambo* will be consulted. These shamans then either speak to the dead themselves or will arrange for a ceremony during which the ancestral spirits can contact their children.

It is much easier with Papa God. (God is always referred to by the Haitian peasant as "Bon Dieu" or "Papa Bon Dieu.") Papa God created the world, but then he sat back and let things run themselves. He makes few demands on his children, but he has his dignity and likes to be treated with proper respect and gratitude. In the folktales he is actually very human—eating, sleeping, smoking, making mistakes. I found him very appealing and often asked storytellers if they knew any stories about Papa God.

Antoine Exavier told two stories about Papa

66

God: "Cat and Dog" and "Papa God and General Death." He told both of them on the same evening, as we were sitting on a stone ledge in Diquini behind the house of his employer, Madame Bellande. Antoine was on very good terms with Madame Bellande. She was more than eighty years old and he was past sixty. He had worked for her for forty years, following her when she moved from her large family farm in Jacmel to Diquini. Diquini was in the countryside even though it was only ten miles from Port-au-Prince. Both Antoine and Madame Bellande were filled with earthy humor and merry conversation. Antoine loved the stories he told and would burst out laughing before the funny parts.

ONE evening Cat and Dog were sitting together by the fire discussing the problems of the village. The hours passed, and Dog turned the conversation to his own concerns.

"If only there were more people," Dog said. "Then I would have much more to eat."

"More people!" Cat exclaimed. "There is not enough food for everyone now. What would happen if more people came?"

"If more people came, there would be more food eaten, and more bones for me!" Dog answered. At the thought of it, his eyes glowed. "Bones . . ." he repeated, smiling. Then he leaped into the air. "That's it. That's how to get more people. I shall go to Papa God and ask him to bring back the dead to fill up the earth."

"Fill up the earth! Dog, there are already people living wherever you can see. Where will they go?"

"Well," Dog considered. "If everyone is forever mourning the dead, they ought to be able to make room for those they miss so much. Yes. My idea is a very good one. I shall visit Papa God tomorrow."

The next morning, Cat was first in line at the butcher's. He bought eight large bones and started on his way to Papa God's house.

En route he dropped the bones in places Dog would be certain to notice.

Cat knocked on Papa God's door. No answer. He put his ear to the door. zzzz . . zzzz . . . . .

"Papa God! Papa God!" he called.

When at last Papa God came to the door, Cat bowed politely three times and explained, "Papa God, I have come to warn you of some recent foolish talk on earth. Dog has been thinking of inviting the dead back. But the truth is, there are already so many people there is not much left to eat, nor much space to live. I know you like your peace and quiet (especially in the mornings), and if the dead return, there will be so much expansion that they'll soon be building houses near you. And certain people can be quite noisy, especially the dead, since they've been quiet for so long."

"Well, well," Papa God said, "sit down and have some coffee."

While Cat sipped his coffee, Papa God thought about how much he enjoyed sleeping late in the mornings. Cat finished his coffee, bowed again politely, and set off for home.

Not until evening did Dog arrive. He had eaten all eight bones and looked twice as fat as in the morning. Papa God was sitting on the porch. Dog tried to bow, but he was so stuffed he could only nod his head.

"Papa God," Dog began, "since you made me without teaching me a trade, it is through the kindness of the people on earth that I eat. I have come to ask you to allow the dead to return to earth so there will be more food and more—"

"More!" Papa God echoed. "MORE! I have never seen such a fat dog as you. Go back home and be glad there is someone who is feeding you so well."

It was only then that Dog realized who might have left all those bones on the way to Papa God's house. It was too late. Dog bowed as best he could to Papa God and went home.

Since that time, the dead have never returned to the earth, nor has Dog ever confided in Cat again.

The One Who
Would Not Listen
to His Own Dream

The One Who Would Not Listen to His Own Dream

About the Story: In Haiti, Catholics, Voodooists, and Protestants take seriously the messages in their dreams. Once, I hired a jeep to drive to Jacmel. The driver arrived on time and was eager to leave. But I was feeling out-of-sorts. It had rained recently, and I kept asking the driver about the condition of the mountain roads. He assured me that the roads were fine and that the sooner we started the better. Finally I told him that I had had a bad dream the night before.

"Oh, no!" the Protestant driver declared. "Then we won't go. It would be too dangerous."

"Why is that?" I asked him.

"Well, it depends on your dream. Tell me your dream."

I had dreamt that I was trying to hide from a man and woman who were standing on a hill looking at me through the window. But each time I would try to seal the blinds with Scotch tape, they would open from another part. I asked the women in the room to cover the windows so that no light would shine out, but the women wanted to be able to admire themselves in the mirror. Then I saw a page with letters arranged in syllables—JAL OF NE FB. I became more and more frightened, for I felt someone could arrange my fate by combining the syllables.

"Oh, that's fine," the driver assured me and started up the motor of the jeep. "As long as no sickness or death came to you in your dream, there is no danger. We can leave for Jacmel."

Jacques, a nineteen-year-old student, told "The One Who Would Not Listen to His Own Dream." He sat on Jeanne Philippe's porch and spoke in a simple, undramatic fashion, as if he were reciting a rote passage.

ONCE, two friends were walking across the countryside. They were both very poor and thought that if they settled in another village, their fortunes might change.

They walked across land, over sand, over stone, over water. Day after day they walked, until one of the friends could go no farther and lay down to rest. The other continued. He walked up a small hill and finally he too lay down to sleep under an orange tree.

As he slept, he dreamt and in his dream a voice came to him and said, "The princess is ill. Take a leaf from the orange tree, make a tea with it, and she will be cured."

When the man woke in the morning, he broke off a large leaf from the tree and continued on his way. In the next town he came to the king's house. On the door of the house was a sign: *Quiet! The princess is ill.*

He knocked on the door and the king answered it.

"Honor, I have come to cure the princess."

"My dear sir," said the king, "if the great doctors in Haiti have not been able to cure her, how will a poor man like you do it?"

"That is why I have come."

The king had no answer to that so he let him in. The young man went to the princess's room. He divided the orange leaf into many tiny

73

pieces. For three days and three nights he spoon-fed orange-leaf tea to the princess, and at the end of that time she was cured.

The king was so pleased he gave the young man three-quarters of his fortune, and the princess and the young man were married. The man lived happily with the princess and she with him. But he had a good memory and did not forget his friend.

After a time he traveled over the mountains to the village where he had last seen his friend. He asked for him and soon found him. The friend was as poor as when they had separated. The man then told his friend all that had happened to him, how he had continued on and fallen asleep under an orange tree, how a voice had come to him, telling him how he might cure the princess, and how he was now married to the princess. At the end of his story, he gave his friend a large sack with gold and wished him well. Then he went home to his wife.

But the friend was not satisfied. He thought to himself: "If he can hear voices, so can I." He walked to the hill his friend had described and lay down under the same orange tree.

He fell asleep. During the night a voice came to him and said, "Go away." But the man only turned over. The voice spoke to him again. "Go away," it said. But the man would not listen. A third time the voice warned him: "Go away."

The man would not listen to his own dream. He stayed. And in the morning he was found, eaten by wild dogs, demons, and *loup-garou.**

* *Loup-garou* is pronounced "lu garu." The peasants in Haiti believe that at night certain members of the community, relatives as well as neighbors, turn into animals and wild creatures and wander the countryside causing evil and working spells. The worst name for them is *loup-garou* (wolf-monsters). They are also called demons and bad spirits.

Papa God and
General Death

Papa God and General Death

About the Story: One day when my daughter Rachel and I were visiting Odette and Milo Rigaud at their home near Pétionville, Rachel went into the bathroom. She was four years old, the Washing Hands Age, and could easily spend an hour washing and rewashing. Suddenly I heard a shriek.

Rachel and Milo both emerged from the bathroom with red faces. Rachel was mortified: she had been stopped just as she was about to wash her face. Milo was horrified: Rachel had used up the family's three days' water allotment for flushing the toilet, bathing, and brushing their teeth.

Rationing the water supply in Port-au-Prince is a frequent occurrence, especially in the dry months between December and March. In the countryside, water is always rationed. In the areas with irrigation systems, each farmer is allowed only a few hours a day for his fields, and it is well known that the controller of irrigation is usually the richest man in the district, more highly paid than the mayor, the judge, or the chief of police. In many mountains and plains areas, no irrigation systems are available; the people are forced to walk every day to the nearest water source, which could be five or ten miles away, depending on where they live.

Antoine Exavier, who farmed the land all his life and knew well the importance of water, told this story to Madame Bellande, and her two great-grandchildren at Madame Bellande's house in Diquini.

ONE evening, two men were walking on a hillside, Papa God and General Death.

As they walked along, General Death pointed to a large yellow stone house overlooking the valley and said, "Last week I took one from there." Then he pointed to a smaller house down the path: "Tomorrow I shall take one from there."

"You are always taking from people," said Papa God, "and I am always giving to them. That is why the people prefer me."

"Oh, I wouldn't be so certain of that," said General Death.

"Well, let's see," said Papa God. "Let's ask the man you will be visiting tomorrow for some water and see whether he gives more water to you or to me."

So Papa God walked up the path to the small house and Death stood waiting by the road.

"Good evening," Papa God called from outside the gate. "Have you some water for a thirsty man?"

"I haven't a drop," the man answered.

"I beg of you," said Papa God. "I am very thirsty. And I am sure Papa God would be pleased if you would give me some water."

"My good fellow, don't talk to me of Papa God. Do you know how far I have to go for water? Ten miles! Five miles to the spring and five miles back! And Papa God makes places where there is so much water people are swimming in it. No, don't talk to me of Papa God."

"My good man," Papa God said patiently, "if you knew with whom you are speaking, I am certain you would give me some water."

"Who are you?" asked the man.

"I—I am Papa God."

"Papa God," said the man, "I still do not have any water. But I will tell you this: if General Death should pass this way, then I would have water."

"How is that?" asked God.

"Because Death has no favorites. Rich, poor, young, old—they are all the same to him. Last week, he took the owner of the large house on the hill, the week before he took my neighbor's wife, the week before a young baby, and the week before that an old man. Death takes from all the houses. But you, you give all the water to some people and leave me here with ten miles to go on my donkey for just one drop."

Papa God saw Death motioning to him. It was Death's turn. Shaking his head sadly, Papa God walked away.

Several minutes later, General Death walked up the path.

"Good evening," he said. "Can you give me some water?"

"If you please," said the man, "what is your name?"

"I am General Death."

The man excused himself and went into his house. He returned with a calabash full of cool water.

"Drink!" he said to General Death. "Drink as much as you wish."

And Death drank. He drank long and he drank fully. And he must have been pleased, for the next day he did not stop at the small house but continued on his route down the hill.

Bouki Dances
the Kokioko

Bouki Dances
the Kokioko

About the Story: Edouard, a farmer from Carrefour-Dufort, called *cric?* as Dadi finished her three-eggs story. He spoke in a rather garbled way and laughed so hard through most of the story that it was often necessary to ask him to repeat certain sentences. When he danced the first part of the kokioko, he held himself erect, his right hand under his right breast, and swayed his upper chest from side to side—a bit like a rooster. When he came to the "Samba dance" section of the song, he clapped and turned around and around. The audience joined him on "Samba dance," singing and clapping while Edouard turned in a circle.

THERE was once a king of Haiti who loved dancing. He loved dancing more than anything else in the world. If he could, he would have invited dancers to perform for him every evening of the week; but unfortunately, he did not have enough money in his treasury to pay them.

One evening after dinner, when the king was sitting alone in his garden, he made up a song:*

* See music p. 200–201.

> Kokioko, oh, Samba,*
> Now I dance, now I dance like this.
> Samba, oh, Samba, ah.
> Now I dance, now I dance like this.
> Samba dance, Samba dance, Samba dance,
>   Samba dance.

He sang it several times, then he stood up. He sniffed the soft night air and, swaying from side to side, he made up a dance to match his song:

> Kokioko, oh, Samba,
> Now I dance, now I dance like this.
> Samba, oh, Samba, ah.
> Now I dance, now I dance like this.
> Samba dance, Samba dance, Samba dance,
>   Samba dance.

And the more he whirled around the more impressed he was with his own dance. "No one could make up such a dance," he thought to himself. "But, of course, there are always those who think they can do anything. Maybe . . ."

The next morning, the king announced that he would pay 5,000 gourdes to anyone who could dance the kokioko. That evening, a long line of dancers, many with newly made amulets around their necks, waited outside the palace hoping they might be able to guess the steps of the kokioko. And that night, the king saw some of the most splendid dancing he had ever seen all for free, for no one, amulet or no amulet, was able to guess the steps of the kokioko.

The next night it was the same thing, and the night after. Sometimes one dancer would happen to do the first steps of the kokioko, and the king would sit up in excitement. Once, a dancer did the first and second parts of the kokioko, but then he did the wrong steps for the Samba dance.

* Samba is a word of African origin meaning master musician or storyteller.

Months passed and the king never tired of watching the dancing. But always after the dancers and servants left for the evening, the king would dance the kokioko by himself, so he wouldn't forget it.

It happened that one evening, Malice, the king's gardener, returned to the palace for his hat. As he came near the garden he heard the king singing:

Kokioko, oh, Samba,
Now I dance, now I dance like this.
Samba, oh, Samba, ah.
Now I dance, now I dance like this.
Samba dance, Samba dance, Samba dance,
Samba dance. . . .

Malice crept up to the gate and saw the king was dancing the kokioko in the moonlight. He followed every movement with greedy eager eyes and then ran home to tell his wife, Madame Malice.

Before work the next morning, Malice went to see his friend, Bouki.

"Bouki," he said, "we have been friends for many years and now I am going to do something *really* great for you."

"Oh-oh," said Bouki. He had been friends long enough with Malice to know that when Malice started out to help you . . . you were much better off *before* he came along. No one was trickier than Malice. "Leave well enough alone!" said Bouki.

"Bouki, do you know what I saw last night? I saw the king dancing the kokioko in his garden. I saw every step he made. I can't dance it for him because I am his servant and he would suspect me. But I will teach you the steps and you will win the 5,000 gourdes."

Now 5,000 gourdes is a lot of money—especially for Bouki, who had many little Boukis to feed. And also for Malice—who had many little Malices.

"Show me the dance," said Bouki.

Malice sang and danced:

Elsa Henriquez

Kokioko, oh, Samba,
Now I dance, now I dance like this.
Samba, oh, Samba, ah.
Now I dance, now I dance like this.
Samba dance, Samba dance, Samba dance,
Samba dance.

Then Bouki tried to follow Malice's movements:

Koki-o-o- OH!

Bouki was so fat and awkward, he nearly fell over.

"Never mind," said Malice. "I'll be back tonight to teach you. We'll do a little bit every night and you'll learn."

Two months later, Bouki and Malice joined the line of dancers waiting outside the king's palace. When it was Bouki's turn, he went in alone and danced for the king. It was a very fat dancer who danced the kokioko, but it *was* the kokioko!

Kokioko, oh, Samba,
Now I dance, now I dance like this.
Samba, oh, Samba, ah.
Now I dance, now I dance like this.
Samba dance, Samba dance, Samba dance,
Samba dance.

There was no doubt about it. The king was flabbergasted, amazed, stunned, and forced to give Bouki his reward. Bouki rushed joyously out of the palace with his sack of 5,000 gourdes.

"I've won, Malice, I've won!" Bouki shouted.

Bouki and Malice walked gaily home through the forest, but as they passed a large breadfruit tree, Malice suddenly stopped and said: "Bouki, now that you can dance the kokioko, I'm going to teach you one of the easiest dances there is."

Malice moved his rump back and forth, closed his eyes and sang:*

* See music p. 203.

> If you have no sense,
> Put your sack on the ground
> And dance.

"That's easy," said Bouki. And he put his sack on the ground and imitated Malice:

> If you have no sense,
> Put your sack on the ground
> And dance.

"Good," said Malice. And he began to sing faster and faster and shake his whole body:

> If you have no sense,
> Put your sack on the ground
> And dance.

Bouki did the same. And his eyes were shut tight when Madame Malice crept out from behind the breadfruit tree and picked up his sack.

> If you have no sense,
> Put your sack on the ground
> And dance.

Suddenly Bouki opened his eyes and looked on the ground. "My *sack*, Malice, my SACK!"

"Oh-oh, did you put it on the gr-round?" asked Malice in mock seriousness.

"Yes, of course."

"Oh, Bouki, no! I *tried* to warn you," said Malice. And he disappeared into the night, singing:

> If you have no sense,
> Put your sack on the ground
> And dance.

Papa God Sends
Turtle Doves

Papa God Sends Turtle Doves

About the Story: Dadi told this story in front of her house in Carrefour-Dufort. The full moon shone behind her as she described the flight of the birds (*Pee O lay*) in the sky. She stood on tiptoes and her arms formed circles above her head, each arm rotating outward from the center of her body. As the intensity of the story increased, her circles became smaller and faster. When the birds turned and turned she used her right arm only and very quickly rotated it in front of her chest in a clockwise motion, with a bent elbow. She spoke the words "turn and turn and turn" in one breath and stopped when her breath gave out. It was a very dramatic and touching storytelling.

THERE was once an old man and an old woman who had three sons. When the sons were not quite grown up, they left their mother and father and went to the city to find work. One went to Jacmel, another went to Mirogoane, and a third went to Port-au-Prince. The father did not want them to go, but the mother said there was not enough food for them all.

Both the mother and father missed their sons. In the mornings they spoke about them and in the evenings they spoke about them.

One morning, when they were particularly lonely for their sons, a turtle dove flew into the courtyard.

"Look, Mother," the old man said, "a turtle dove."

"Yes," the woman said. "It makes me think of our children."

"Papa God has sent us this turtle dove, let us take care of him."

"Why does it make me think of my children, I wonder," said the old woman and she shook her head sadly.

But the old man did not wonder. He went into the fields and came back with some wood with which he made a cage for the turtle dove. He gave the bird grain and water and the bird stayed.

The next morning, the old couple found a second turtle dove in their yard.

"Look, Mother," the old man said. "Papa God has sent us another turtle dove to keep our first turtle dove company."

"When I look at it, it makes me think of our sons. I don't want it here," the old woman said.

But the father put it in the cage with the first turtle dove. And the next morning, a third turtle dove landed in their yard.

"Mother, see, now it is finished. We have the third. Our sons are home with us again."

"What are you talking about?"

"Yes, they left as children and returned as birds."

"How can children leave and return as birds? I never heard of such a thing."

"Old woman, don't you know God can do whatever he wishes?"

"I want my children, not these birds!" the woman screamed. She seized one of the birds by the neck as if she would kill it.

"If you hurt that bird you will hurt yourself," the father said. "If you don't believe me, look at your left breast."

The woman looked down at herself and saw three drops of blood on her breast.

"I have warned you. Now let the birds be." And the father went into the fields to work.

But the woman could not stand the sight of the birds. All day she went in and out of the house and tried to avoid looking at the birds, but a fury got into her and she seized one from the cage and brought it into the house and killed it.

At that moment in the fields, the father heard his son calling him and turned around. Outlined against the evening sky was the image of his son.

"Papa, Mama has killed me," he said.

"That is nonsense," the father said. "You have been away for ten years and now you say your mother has killed you."

"But you know I am back. You yourself said so."

Then the father ran toward the house and saw one of the birds was missing from the cage. He went inside and truly the mother had killed it. She had cooked it in a pot and now she put it in a plate for him to eat. But he could not eat it. He brought it outside and laid it on the ground while he opened the door of the cage. "Fly away," he said to the other birds, "fly away."

But the birds flew down to the earth, and gathering the bones of the turtle dove from the plate, they flew up into the air. *Pee o lay. Pee o lay.* They circled and circled in the air, and the man and woman saw there were three turtle doves flying.

Pee o lay. Pee o lay. Pee o lay. One of the turtle doves fluttered down into the woman's face and said, "Look at me fly, Mama." *Pee o lay. Pee o lay. Pee o lay. Pee o lay. Pee o lay.* "I'm flying for you." And the bird made greater and greater circles in the sky.

The second bird fluttered in the face of the father and said, "Look at me fly, Papa. I'm flying for you." *Pee o lay. Pee o lay. Pee o lay. Pee o lay. Pee o lay.*

Then the third bird flew toward the mother and said, "Why did you want to kill me? Didn't you know we would return to you?"

Then all three birds began to turn in the air, to turn and turn and turn and turn and turn and turn and turn and turn and turn . . . until they fell to the ground. And there stood the old man and woman's three sons. When the mother saw them, she dropped down dead.

They tried to bring her back to life, but it was too much for her to believe that children could leave and return as birds. It was not too much for the father. And he and his three sons lived happily together until the end of their lives.

The Singing Bone

The Singing Bone

About the Story: Late one afternoon, as I sat by the river in Carrefour-Dufort, watching the sun set and waiting until the work in the sugar-cane fields would be over, a few young women and older boys gathered around me. We were chatting together when an unkempt woman with few teeth, torn clothes, and an angry look approached from the river bank.

"What do you have in there?" She was referring to my blue canvas bag. I opened it wide so she could see the contents: a black tape recorder, pens and pencils, a tan notebook. "Give it to me," she said, pointing to the tape recorder.

"I need it," I answered.

"I need it more," she said. "You are rich. You are a foreigner. I am poor." She touched her own thin clothes to demonstrate her words. "Give it to me," she repeated.

"No," I finally answered.

"Then give me money," she said.

I looked at the people around me. They all needed money. One of the younger boys joined her: "Give *me* money, come on." I looked for Willy, but as usual, he had disappeared. The woman grabbed at my skirt. The younger boys surrounded me.

I had told no one at the hotel where I was going. I realized that no one knew where I was. Rachel would soon be going to sleep in Port-au-Prince. I stood up. "Okay," I said, "if you tell me a story, a good story, I'll pay you."

She burst out laughing. She spit on the ground and waved her arms crazily at me. Then she stormed off, shouting and sputtering epithets.

I stood watching her until she reached the bend in the river. I sat down. No one said anything. After a while the talk resumed. I waited until the voices of the others became loud and bright, then I leaned toward the tall young man sitting on my left and lowered my voice. "Are there any police in Carrefour-Dufort?" I asked him.

"Yes," he answered. "I'm the police."

I looked at him more closely. It must be true: he was the only one in the crowd whose clothes had no rips or patches. He was wearing a new straw hat. He was the police.

News of my meeting with the woman spread through the community. I, who had arrived in the afternoon so in control, was by evening turned about. I sat at the evening's storytelling feeling vulnerable and open to whatever was to be.

That evening Justine told "The Singing Bone." Swamé, a laborer of fifty, gave a full-length rendition of "The Gizzard." The moon was full, the frogs croaking, the children loud and noisy. A spark was running from storyteller to storyteller: everyone wanted to tell. It was one of the most lively evenings in Carrefour-Dufort. It was also the first time a storyteller offered me a role in her story. When the father in "The Singing Bone" asked the king if he would take his bet, Justine put out her hand to me. "Cut!" she said. I put out my hand to her. "Cut!" the others answered for me. We touched hands. The bet was on.

Yet, despite the full support the audience gave Justine during her story, when she came to the moral, a man shouted, "It is not for you to draw those morals." Justine was under twenty, outspoken, and independent in her ways. She would not be silenced. She shouted back at him: "I have as much right as you!"

"Yes!" her friends cried. "She told the story well."

"No, no," the others protested, "not for a loose woman—"

But before the argument could get underway, another storyteller cried "*Cric?*" and there were sufficient *cracs* for the story to begin. Story after story, I was learning: A story begins much before its beginning.

THERE was once a man who didn't have much luck with women. His first wife died leaving him with a small boy. He married again and had another son. Then his second wife died. When he married a third time he chose a woman who was very fat and very mean. It seemed like she'd live a long time.

One day she said to her two stepsons, "Whoever brings me the largest bundle of firewood shall have the most to eat at dinner."

Out the door ran the older boy. The younger boy started to follow, but before he could reach the door, the stepmother took a hard cane stick and hit him over the head and killed him. Then she put the kettle on the fire to boil. She cut the boy into pieces and threw him into the pot.

When the older boy returned with firewood, she told him to bring his father his dinner. The boy carried the plate to his father's shop. The father went out into the yard and ate his dinner. Only one bone remained. This the father threw under an orange tree. Then he went back to work.

Before the brother returned, he looked around the yard for more wood. As he passed near the orange tree, the bone underneath it began to sing: *

> Oh brother mine, come close to me,
> Oh brother mine, listen now to me:
> Stepmother killed me
> Father ate me
> Here I lie
> Under the orange tree.

"Oh-oh." The boy ran into his father's shop.

"Father, come quick," he cried, "there is a bone singing in the garden."

"Son, how can a bone sing?"

"Truly, Father, the bone *is* singing. Come with me and you will hear for yourself."

The father followed his son, and when the boy came close to the tree, the bone began to sing:

> Oh brother mine, come close to me,
> Oh brother mine, listen now to me:
> Stepmother killed me
> Father ate me
> Here I lie
> Under the orange tree.

"Oh-oh. The bone truly sings," said the father, "and I have found my fortune." He picked up the bone and put it in his belt. He did not return to work, but went home.

"Look here, wife," he said. "I have in my belt a bone that can sing."

When the wife saw the bone, she looked quickly away and asked the boy if he wanted to eat.

* See music p. 204–205.

"No, I shall wait for my brother."

"Silly," the stepmother said. "He is out playing. You know how little ones are, as long as their bellies are full they will continue to play. Come now, eat."

"No," the boy insisted. "I shall wait for my brother."

"Let us leave now for the king," said the father. "With this bone I shall make my fortune."

As the family approached the palace, they saw the king sitting in his garden sharing a barbecue with some of his friends.

"King," the father said, "I have come to make a bet with you. I own a bone that knows how to sing."

"Where have you found such a marvel?" asked the king.

"No matter," the father answered. "Do you take my bet?"

"Cut," said the king.

"Cut," said the father.

"I take your bet. Now let us see your bone."

The father took the bone from his belt and placed it on the ground. "Go up to the bone," he said to the king, "and you will hear it sing."

The king went up to the bone, but the bone did not sing.

The father went up to the bone, but the bone did not sing.

The stepmother went up to the bone, but the bone did not sing.

When the brother went up to the bone, the bone sang:

> Oh brother mine, come close to me,
> Oh brother mine, listen now to me:
> Stepmother killed me
> Father ate me
> Here I lie
> Under the orange tree.

"I begin to understand," said the king. "You own a singing bone, but tell me, how many sons do you have?"

"Two."

"I only see one here," said the king. "Send for the other."

Messengers were sent to look for the boy, but no one had seen him.

"I understand even better now," said the king. And he sent his servants into the palace to bring out the largest cooking pot in the kitchen.

"Now then," he said to the stepmother, "go up to the bone and let us hear it sing."

She went up to the bone, but the bone did not sing.

"Go over to the fire instead," he ordered her.

"Son, go up to the bone," the king said to the boy.

The brother went up to the bone and the bone sang:

> Oh brother mine, come close to me,
> Oh brother mine, listen now to me:
> Stepmother killed me
> Father ate me
> Here I lie
> Under the orange tree.

And while the king listened to the bone singing, he noticed that the stepmother, standing next to the fire, was beginning to melt.

"Do not lose all that good fat," said the king. "Put her into the cooking platter and put the cooking platter over the fire."

The fire blazed and the stepmother melted and melted and melted. She melted, until she was all gone.

The king picked up the bone and brought it over to the platter. He slowly greased the bone and the bone began to grow: feet, legs, organs, stomach, chest, arms, neck, mouth, nose, eyes, hair—and there the boy stood, just as he had been.

"So," said the king to the father, "you did not win the bet. For you no longer have a singing bone, but you have your two sons again. And now I say to all who are here: Choose whom you want to marry, but if you choose a tree that has fruit, you must care for the fruit as much as for the tree."

The Gizzard

The Gizzard

About the Story: At the end of the storytelling evening in Carrefour-Dufort, Swamé began his story of "The Gizzard." The other storytellers that evening had stood and moved about. There had been much dancing and singing. But Swamé sat on a chair, and looking straight at me, spoke quietly without stopping. By then it was eleven o'clock. The audience was tired and restless. They were farmers who rise with the sun at four in the morning. "That's enough!" someone called out. "Stop!" People began to mill about and talk loudly. Others continued to shout for Swamé to finish: "Too long! Enough!" But Swamé continued, undaunted, to the end.

In Swamé's story of "The Gizzard," the *hungan* (pronounced hoon-gahn) appears in three different roles: the *hungan*-diviner who uses cards; the *hungan*, man of wealth, who needs no charity; and the *hungan* as healer. In the early days the *hungan* or *mambo* (female Priestess) grew into their positions with age or knowledge. These people were in direct contact with their family spirits and cured family members of their illnesses. They did not claim to be *hungans*, only servants of the spirits, and they usually worked at other trades to earn money. The modern *hungan*, who is concerned principally with healing the sick, is in this tradition. *Hungan*-healer, he is known as the *hungan-makout* because of the straw bag he carries over his shoulder, which contains his herbs and medicaments.

There is another *hungan* now, the *hungan-asson*. He has bought his powers from spirits who are not his family spirits. With his arrival there is more black magic and sorcery. He always uses an *asson*, a gourde rattle made from snakebones, in performing his ceremonies. It is from this rattle that his powers derive, for he obtained it during his own initiation ceremonies.

When the princess in "The Gizzard" goes to see a *hungan*, it is probably a *hungan-asson*. She follows the usual procedure. She brings with her payment, normally a bottle of clairin and a candle, but as she is a princess, three sacks of silver is quite fitting. The *hungan* then divines why she has come, either by reading cards or by a candle flame held over a tin of water. The princess chooses cards and wisely waits for his divination of her problem. She then pays him for his diagnosis. If she had come to be treated for illness, she would have had to return another time or to have consulted another *hungan*, probably a *hungan-makout*, who would be involved in the curing ceremonies.

On my next visit to Haiti, I was eager to hear more stories from Swamé. Willy and I drove to Carrefour-Dufort, but Swamé wasn't there. We were told he had gone to the Dominican Republic to find work cutting sugar cane. The next year I came to Haiti, I again asked for Swamé. He was in Haiti, but not then in Carrefour-Dufort. Friends of his assured me they could find him. I said I would return in three days.

At last I was seated in a straw chair in Carrefour-Dufort, two feet away from Swamé. I offered Swamé a present and thanked him for the story of

"The Gizzard." I said I could not forget it and asked if he would tell another such long, beautiful story.

Swamé refused the present. He said he would not tell a story unless I gave him five dollars. Willy removed his glasses in a grand gesture of amazement. Five dollars is almost a week's salary in Haiti! Would it be proper for me to pay Swamé five dollars for *one* story? Willy would call me a fool. But then, I thought, how is it possible to put a price on a story, especially from a man who can tell such a story as "The Gizzard"?

Swamé began, but within the first two sentences, he got confused. The others said no, that wasn't the way the story went. Swamé began another story. Again the others corrected him. He tried three or four times, but he could not tell a story.

Cric? someone called. The stories went their round. Then I turned to Swamé. And again he began, and again he became confused.

I had not realized how true it was: A story has no price. It is a gift of the spirit. It comes of the moment. It is here and it is gone.

For whatever reasons, Swamé could not duplicate what he had done three years before. His head was determined. He was eager to try. But his spirit refused.

THERE was once a mother who had three sons. She was very poor and worked all the time. But one day she stopped for a moment and said to herself: "I do not have three boys so that I can do all the work. They must work too. They must have some trade. Yet it would make no sense for me to choose a trade for them without asking them."

So she called her oldest boy to her and said to him: "My child, what trade would you like to do?"

"Mama," he answered, "I would like to be a sailor, working on the sea."

"I shall send you there," she said and called her second son.

"Mama, I would like to be a carpenter," he said. The mother agreed and called her third son.

"My child, what trade would you like?"

"Mama, what I would like most in the world is to walk in the fields and hunt and take what the Good Lord gives me."

The mother agreed. She sent her oldest son off to the sea. She apprenticed her second son to a carpenter, and the youngest son lived at home.

In the mornings, the youngest son would rise early and take his gun and go hunting. Sometimes he returned that evening, sometimes the next night, but he always brought back food for himself and his mother.

It must have been that the Good Lord approved of hunting as the trade for the third son. It seemed especially so as, within the next year, the first son was drowned at sea and the second son was killed at work by a hammer, leaving only the third son to live at home and fight with his mother against poverty.

One morning, the boy woke up early and left for the woods. When he was high in the hills, he saw a small, pretty bird with a mark of pink under the neck. The bird was beautiful, so beautiful, the boy said to himself: "How can I kill this little bird? But then, how can I not kill it? Isn't hunting the trade the Good Lord gave me?"

The boy took his gun and aimed at the bird and shot it. The bird fell to the ground as if dead. But it wasn't dead, for the boy had shot it, not to kill it, but to graze it. He ran to the bird and picked it up and stroked it gently. He talked to it and caressed its feathers, and then he blew lightly under its feathers. *Whh h h*. And the bird revived.

The boy took the bird home and said to his mother: "Mama, all the animals I bring you are for us to eat. But you must never eat this bird. Even if you are dying of hunger, you must never eat it. We must respect this bird and consider it different."

The boy made a cage for the bird and bought some grain. Before he left in the morning he fed the bird and told his mother to feed the bird again at eleven o'clock and to give the bird as much grain as it wanted. The bird grew and became beautiful. It groomed itself and cleaned its feathers and looked very much like a pigeon.

One morning a white man was driving in his car past the house and saw the bird in its cage. He immediately recognized the pink marking under the throat where the gizzard was. This was a special bird, and anyone who would eat its gizzard would become so rich that his house would fill to the ceiling with silver.

It didn't take the man long to stop his car and go through the gate and knock on the woman's door.

"Madame," he said, "may I ask you for a glass of water?"

Oh, these white people, they were always needing special things. Knives, forks, spoons, glasses. She didn't own any glasses.

"Excuse me," she said, "I will have to go next door to my neighbor and borrow a glass—"

"No, no," said the man. "I only want a little water to clear my throat."

The woman then offered him the jug. He poured some water into a cup, swished it around in his mouth and spit it out.

"Madame," he said, "I did not come to you because I needed water, but rather because I saw how poor you are and I have come to make a bargain with you. I would like to eat the gizzard of that little bird in the courtyard. If you will kill it and cook it for me, the minute I eat it, I shall marry you."

Oh! The woman nearly became crazy. She ran here and there telling everyone that she was getting married! Then the white man put his hand in his pocket and took out a fifty-dollar bill.

"Buy whatever is needed," he said. "Tomorrow we are getting married."

The woman hurried to buy chickens, beans, rice, and bananas. She invited everyone she knew. Early the next morning she bought a small pot with three legs. She killed the bird and set it to cook in the pot in the courtyard. She stayed in the house busying herself preparing all the dishes for the guests.

It must have been that the Good Lord was watching out for that boy, for he decided to stop hunting and return home. As he walked down the street he heard people talking about his mother. "She is going to marry a rich man!"

"What difference does it make?" he thought to himself. "If you are not born to be rich, you never will be."

Still, as he came near his house and saw so many people standing around, he wondered why his mother had not told him, not even one word, about getting married. He entered the courtyard and saw some meat cooking in a small pot with three legs. He reached in the pot and took a small piece. He didn't even know what it was. Plop. He swallowed it. Then he left.

What had he eaten? The gizzard, of course!

Some of the guests were standing around the table, some were seated. Soon the white man came in and sat down in front of a plate that had been especially prepared for him. He examined the meat, poking here and there. He could not find the gizzard. He stood up and said: "Madame, there will be no marriage."

Plop. Madame fainted. Fortunately there was Four Flowers Vinegar in the house, which someone found and poured into her ear and she woke up.

"Madame," said the white man, "there was no gizzard in the small bird and that was what I needed. I am therefore not obliged to marry you."

The man walked out of the house and got into his car. Madame ran after him and saw her son coming up the street.

"Child," she cried. "Did you take anything that was cooking in the three-legged pot in the courtyard?"

"Yes, Mama, I just took a small piece—"

Oh-oh. I cannot repeat to you the words that mother then used to her son. But I will tell you that she went into the house, took out everything the boy owned, and threw it on the street.

"Never come back in this courtyard again," she said.

The boy began to cry. He picked up his clothes and things and walked down the street toward the hills. All day he hunted. But in the evening he realized he had no matches to make a fire.

Then in the distance he saw a fire and walked toward its light. He came to a house, entered the courtyard, and knocked on the door. An old woman, who was a witch, answered.

"Old woman," said the boy, "I have been hunting since the afternoon but I have no matches to cook my meat. I saw your fire and have come to ask you if I can use some of your fire to roast my meat."

"Child," said the old woman in a low voice, "you are a small boy. This house is yours, but as for the animals, throw them away. When an old woman prepares dinner, she prepares everything: meat, rice, beans, bananas. Dinner will soon be ready and I will give you your portion."

The boy ate and ate and ate. His stomach grew and grew and grew, until he could not eat any more.

"Little boy," the old woman said, "you will stay with me until you die." She meant that she and her son, who was also a witch, would eat him the next morning. But this was not to be—for this boy was lucky—and things always went well for him.

The next morning when the boy woke up he was covered with silver. The entire floor was covered with silver. Oh. The boy ran to the old woman and told her what had happened. Oh-oh. She ran to the room and saw the silver—all the silver. She scooped it up and after many trips put it all in the trunk in her room.

Then she told her son, and when he saw all the silver in the trunk, he said: "Mother, we cannot eat this boy. We must respect him."

Then he went into the boy's room and hugged him, saying: "We shall be brothers. I am the older and you are the younger."

So the boy lived with the two witches a long time. Every evening his room would fill with silver and soon there were no empty containers in the house. They bought the boy all kinds of clothes. He had more than one hundred pairs of shoes. They gave him such rich food to eat that he became fat. Then they gave him a pair of glasses, even though he didn't need them. But the boy never left the courtyard because the old woman had warned him that there were devils living nearby who would eat him.

Still, as the time passed and the boy grew older, he began to dream of girls. One Sunday, the boy washed himself and put on his finest suit.

He looked at himself in the mirror and said: "The time has come for you to marry." He went to the old woman and said he was going to take a stroll in the courtyard.

As he walked in the courtyard he watched the old woman, and the minute she turned her head—*whoosht*—he was over the gate and into the street. He stopped awhile to catch his breath and collect himself. Then he began to saunter. The boy was dressed in no ordinary costume and he knew it.

He strolled down the street and passed the king's house. Now the king had a daughter who often sat in her balcony watching the men go by. But if any man tried to talk to her, she would never answer. The instant she saw that young man she said: "That one is for me." She sent word to her father that the guards should stop the young man who was passing in the street, for she wanted to marry him and no other, and if she did not marry him, it would be the king's fault. The king immediately sent two strong guards to chase after the young man.

"Mister," they called.

But the young man did not turn to the right or the left. He had gone out to find a woman and those were men who were calling him.

"Mister! Mister!" the guards cried, catching up to him.

The young man looked at them from under his glasses and said: "What is troubling you?" (You know how certain people are when they have a little money. They think they're *so* important.)

"The king has sent for you."

(And you know what that boy said?) "Which king?"

"The king. The king wants to speak with you."

So the young man returned to the king's house.

"Hello, King," he said waving his hand.

The king began to explain at once: "I have a daughter who has fallen in love with you from watching you pass by in the street. She says she will die, and it will be my fault, if she does not marry you. I ask you, for my sake, marry my daughter."

"My dear king, I would be happy to be married, but at the moment I have no money."

"Oh, don't let that trouble you. I have plenty of money."

"Well, if that is how it is, I should like to be married tonight."

You can imagine how many phone calls the king had to make and in so short a time, but everyone was at the wedding that evening.

The next morning when the princess woke up, she saw their room was filled with silver.

"Papa, papa," she went running to her father. "I have married a man richer than you are."

"Nonsense, my child, I am the richest man there is, and should any man be richer than I am, he would be king of all of Haiti."

But the princess insisted that the king come to their room to see for himself. Oh-oh. The floor *was* covered with silver. And every evening, more and more.

It became too much for the princess. And one day she took three sacks of silver, put them in the back seat of her car, and drove out into the country to see a *hungan*. She asked the *hungan* to read her cards.

"Yes, I see," said the *hungan*. "You have come about your husband. He receives money in a magical way."

"Yes, *hungan*. But how?"

"What happens that he receives money like that—what happens —it is the gizzard of a small bird he has swallowed. Even if he dies, the gizzard will still be in his body, and he will receive money, even under the earth. He will receive money all his life."

"*Hungan*, how can I get the gizzard?"

"Have you ever taken a bath with your husband at the holy spring at four o'clock in the morning?"

"No."

"Good. Then ask your husband to do so. And buy yourself a bottle of regurgitive and a bottle of rum."

The husband agreed to take such a bath. And when he stepped out of the holy spring, *brrr* he was chilly.

"Quick, drink this," said the princess. "It will warm you up." But it was the regurgitive she gave him. And it made him throw up. The third time, out came the gizzard. The princess grabbed it up and swallowed it. Then they both drank several glasses of rum and went home.

When they woke in the morning, it was the princess who was rich and the young man who was poor. How long did she allow him to stay? Two days. Then he was sent away.

The grand young man walked in the streets. He still had friends who invited him to eat and drink, to dances and parties. But as he had only one suit, the more he wore it, the more shabby it became, and soon it had holes, and then he was truly poor. He developed an infection in his eyes. Then he became blind. He walked along, with his eyes closed, his hand out, asking: "Give charity to a poor man." He was so poor he didn't even have a young child to guide him.

Once, as he was walking up a small hill, he said to himself, "I am tired. I shall find a tree and lie down in the shade." He soon fell asleep. Plop! Something fell and hit him on the face.

"Ah," he said, "I must have been sleeping under a mango tree."

He reached for his cane and slid it along the earth looking for the mango. *Tok.* The cane struck something. He reached down, picked it up and ate it.

"Why this isn't a mango," he said, "it's an apple. *Good Lord!* I can see. I can see! Thank you, Good Lord. Thank you, life. Now I shall become a *hungan* and never have to ask for charity again."

He picked up the apples under the tree and squeezed their juice into his calabash. Then he noticed another apple tree with even more beautiful apples. He went to that tree and picked an apple and ate it. At first, it tasted delicious, but then he began to feel strange. His eyes hurt. He was blind again.

But then, he rubbed some of the juice from his calabash over his eyes. He could see. He shook apples from the tree that made him blind until he had a great quantity. He walked to the road with the apples and waited for a girl who was returning from the marketplace.

"Young girl," he called out.

The girl ignored him.

"Young girl," he called again. "Look at me, I am in no shape to chase after girls. I am asking you for a favor and one that can help you too."

The girl came closer and listened.

"I want you to sell these apples for me. You can sell them for five dollars or for whatever price you want. Keep the money; I don't want the money. But I want you to sell them at the house of the king, and none other. And should anyone on the way try to buy these apples, you are to refuse. These apples are only for the king's house."

The girl agreed and took the apples. As she walked toward the king's house, several people asked her how much the apples were, but she didn't answer. As soon as she reached the king's house, she called out: "Apples. Foreign apples. Apples." The princess asked her how much she wanted for her apples.

"I am selling them for ten dollars," she said. "They are foreign apples."

She was paid ten dollars.

Everyone ate the apples: the king, the queen, the princess, the children; even the turkeys, they ate the apple pits. And everyone became blind. Fortunately the guards had not eaten the apples so they could help the royal family about. Many of them went all over the country looking for a *hungan* who could cure the royal family, but no one could.

Soon the young man presented himself at the house. He claimed he was a *hungan* and rubbed the juice over the king's eyes. The king could see. Then he put the juice over the eyes of the queen, and the children. They could see again. But he said to the king: "There is something that is preventing the princess from seeing. She needs a bath at the holy spring. I shall take her myself."

And at four o'clock in the morning, when the princess emerged from the spring, he gave her the regurgitive. Out came the gizzard. The young man picked it up and swallowed it. Then he rubbed the juice over her eyes and told her: "You can go."

The king asked him how many thousands of dollars he wanted for having cured them.

"I need no money," he answered, "for I am richer than you are."

Whether he stayed with the royal family or not, I don't know. Whatever he did, wherever he went, he always had money. The boy himself had said: "If you are not born to be rich, you never will be."

But the *hungan* had said: "He will have money all his life."

And he did.

The Monkey
Who Asked
for Misery

The Monkey
Who Asked
for Misery

About the Story: Limène, a farmer and the husband of Dadi, told "The Monkey Who Asked for Misery" to a very delighted and enthusiastic audience at a storytelling gathering in Carrefour-Dufort.

Limène's story of Monkey is in fact one episode in a three-episode story involving Dog, Cat, and Monkey. Limène began: Dog meets Cat walking along the highway and asks him where he has been. "I am walking along and you are walking along," Cat answers. "What need do you have to know where I am coming from? But since you have asked, I will now arrest you, for I am the police." They are soon in a fight, and Cat dirties himself. But Cat is not completely certain it is he that has done so. He therefore goes to a *hungan* to find out whether it was he or Dog. While the *hungan* is performing a ceremony of divination Dog arrives with the same question. Cat leaves and meets Monkey. Monkey advises Cat to go home. At this moment, a woman walks by with a calabash on her head (beginning the episode used in this collection). Monkey forgets Cat and Dog, but at the end, after he is chased by Dog, Monkey, too, dirties himself. In the last episode, Monkey and Dog go to a dance together. They get into a fight over Monkey's candy. Dog insists Monkey give him more. Monkey says he has

114

no more. "Then tell me what it is called," Dog insists. "Monkey-turd," Monkey answers. The episode and story end with more turd and another brawl.

There are hundreds of Haitian stories built around excrement, and every time they are told they are greeted with shouts of joy and merriment. The adults are as eager for and delighted by these stories as the children. Each time I heard one I was entranced at the outset—they almost always begin in a witty, clever manner—but as soon as the word "poupou" or "caca" enters the story, everyone, storyteller included, seems to be so overwhelmed that story line, sense, and wit are abandoned for sheer pleasure at the quantity of times poupou, caca or turd can be mentioned.

MONKEY was sitting in a tree when a woman walked by on her way to market. Just as she passed, she tripped and the calabash on her head fell off and broke. The sweet sugar-cane syrup in the calabash ran all over the ground.

"Good Lord, what Misery you have given me," she cried. "For three days I have been walking to market to sell this syrup and now I've lost it. Good Lord, Papa God, why did you give me such Misery?" But there was nothing to be done, so the woman continued on her way.

Monkey came down from the tree. What was this Misery Papa God had given the woman? He sniffed it. *Hmmm.* It smelled good. He put one finger in and licked it. *Hmm.* He put in another finger. He put in his hand. And then one foot. And soon he was licking it up from the ground. *Th Th Th Th Th . . . Thh.* Then it was gone. But Monkey wanted more. He had not known Misery was so sweet. He decided to visit Papa God. He raced at top speed and found Papa God.

"Good morning, Papa God," said Monkey.

"Hello, Brother Monkey," said Papa God.

"I've come to see you, Papa God."

"Yes, Brother Monkey."

"Papa God—I want Misery."

"In the awful condition you're in, *you* want Misery?"

"Oh yes, Papa God, I need lots and lots and lots of Misery."

"Brother Monkey—"

"Papa God, I've already tasted Misery. I know how sweet it is."

"Well then, go over there. Do you see the three sacks? Take that one. No, not that one—*that* one. Yes. Put it on your back and walk until you come to a place where there are no trees. Then open it up. But remember, if you truly want lots of Misery, there must not be any trees in the place where you open it."

Monkey took the sack. He put it on his back. He thanked Papa God and left. He walked and walked and walked and walked and walked. He walked and walked and at last, he came to a place where there was not one tree to be seen. Monkey set the sack down. He looked in every direction. There was not one tree. He rubbed his stomach. He couldn't wait. He loosened the string of the sack and opened it up.

Rrrrrr. Rrrrr. Rrrrrrrr. Five huge dogs jumped out of the sack and began to chase Monkey. Monkey ran. The dogs followed close behind him. When Monkey had no breath left, a tree appeared. *One* tree. Monkey climbed that tree and the dogs barked and scratched, but they could not reach Monkey.

Papa God had sent the tree. Papa God sent the tree especially to Monkey.

Too much Misery at one time is not a good thing—even for Monkey.

The Name

The Name

About the Story: The woman who told "The Name" was a solid, strong, fierce woman in her forties. She had been a peasant but now lived in a newly built cement house north of Pétionville and owned a grocery store. She spoke in a firm, no-nonsense voice to a group of her relatives and neighborhood children that had gathered in the evening on her porch. Her gestures were cutting, and as I listened to her I was afraid.

After visiting her house the second time, my tape recorder, tapes, and canvas bag suddenly vanished in the night. I had had them when I stepped into my car. They were gone when I reached the hotel. How could they have disappeared? I turned at midnight and drove back to Bois-Moquet. Everyone was surprised. Yes, they had all seen me put everything into the car. How could it have disappeared? Ernst, the hotel manager at the San-Souci, suggested I see either a *hungan* or the mayor in the morning.

The mayor of Pétionville was a gallant, dressed in bright green, and sporting two pistols in his hip pockets. He listened intently as I spoke and then advised me to come back in two weeks when he would have more time. In two weeks, I would be in New York. Fortunately I had thought to bring two tape recorders, so I grieved over the loss of my tapes, and the stories that had been told, but after all, what was to be done?

The next evening, when I was driving with Willy back from Carrefour-Dufort and he heard the story, he insisted justice must be done. So the following morning, Willy and I stood in a crowd of eager plaintiffs at the police station in Port-au-Prince. At last my turn came and I was ushered into a small room. The officer nodded to me and listened seriously as I described each incident. "Yes," he said, but when he picked up his desk phone to investigate, the phone was dead. He called for another phone to be brought in, and that, too, was dead. He looked at me and I at him. We both shrugged our shoulders. I looked at Willy. He was standing in the doorway, but he'd seen. He shrugged his shoulders, too.

I thanked the officer and walked out into the bright sunlit streets of Port-au-Prince. Schoolgirls in their navy blue uniforms and brown oxfords were passing by. Gangly youths dressed as policemen stood at attention outside the gendarmerie. And far up in the mountains, in Bois-Moquet, was the woman who had told "The Name." I could feel her presence here in the city. What defense did the mayor, the police, or even the telephones have against her powers? Her elemental force had to be recognized and reckoned with. After all, was it not the stuff that folktales are made of?

THERE was once a girl who worked for an old woman. Each time the old woman sat down at the table, she said to the girl: "If you tell me my name, I will give you something to eat."

But the girl never said anything, for she did not know the

woman's name. From the time she woke up in the morning until the time she went to sleep, the girl worked for this old woman, cleaning her house, cooking her meals, doing whatever the woman asked. And the woman never gave her anything to eat or drink.

There was no one the girl could go to for help, for all the neighbors had long since moved away. They knew the old woman was a witch.

"Don't blame me if you are hungry," the old woman would say as she sat down at the table. "Tell me my name and I will give you something to eat."

The poor girl remained silent and hungry.

One day the woman bought a large turkey and killed it. She gave the girl the intestines and told her to wash them in the river.

When the girl got to the river with the intestines, the fish, the shrimp, and the eel were waiting for her at the river's edge.

"Little girl," the eel called to her, "if you give me something to eat, I will tell you the name of the old woman."

The girl willingly gave the eel a part of the intestines. *Fwip.** The eel swallowed it and disappeared under the water without saying anything.

"Little girl," called the shrimp, "if you give *me* something to eat, I will tell you the old woman's name."

The girl broke off another piece of the intestines and gave it to the shrimp. *Fwip.* The shrimp swallowed it and disappeared.

"Little girl," said the fish, "give me some of the intestines. I am the one who will tell you the woman's name."

Only a small piece remained. The girl gave almost all of it to the fish. *Fwip.* The fish swallowed it and was off, without saying a word.

All that was left was a little piece, not much bigger than my small finger.

"No one has told me anything," the girl cried. "And now I have to go back to the house and what will I say?"

Then the crab poked his head out from under the sand.

* *Fwip* is an African onomatopoeic sound for swallowing. It is done by keeping your mouth open and making the sound "sh" as you inhale.

"Very good," he said. "Give me what is left and I will tell you the name."

The girl gave the last bit to the crab.

The crab chewed it slowly. After he finished, he said: "Do you know what the old woman is called? Her name is 'In the Storm, Coffin on her Back.' "

"Thank you," said the girl.

"Now, when you return," the crab continued, "wait until the woman is seated at the table and when she asks you what her name is— tell her. But it is not necessary for you to tell the old woman *who* told you her name. If you do, she will come here and try to kill me."

"I won't tell her," the girl promised.

When the girl entered the house, the woman was already seated at the table with her rice and beans and salt and pepper before her.

"Tell me my name," the woman said as always, "and you may have something to eat."

"I know your name," the girl replied.

"Who told you my name?"

"I know your name."

"Tell me."

" 'In the Storm, Coffin on your Back.' "

The woman rose from the table. She was furious. She took the machete from the wall and ran down to the river.

The girl didn't follow her. She sat down in the woman's place and began to eat and eat and eat.

"Eel!" cried the woman. "Did you tell the girl my name?"

"Not me, old woman," said the eel. "It wasn't me."

"Shrimp, did you tell the girl my name?"

"Not me, old woman. It wasn't me."

"Fish, did you tell the girl my name?"

"Not me, old woman," said the fish. "It wasn't me."

The old woman became angrier and angrier. She walked into the water looking for the animal who had told the girl her name. Then she stepped on something and saw it was a crab under her foot.

"Crab!" she cried. "Did you tell the girl my name?"

"Yes, old woman," said the crab, "it was me!" And he started moving backward into the river.

The woman plunged into the water after the crab.

"Crab, did you tell the girl my name?"

"Yes, old woman," answered the crab, moving deeper and deeper into the water. "Yes, old woman, yes. Yes. Yes. Yes. It was me."

"Crab!" shouted the old·woman. And then she slipped on a rock, hit the bottom, and didn't come up again.

"Yes, old woman," said the crab. "It *is* me." And he ate her up, name and all.

Cat's Baptism

Cat's Baptism

About the Story: This storytelling occasion was one of my favorites. I had spent the day with Odette Menesson Rigaud in Kenscoff and we stopped in the late afternoon at the home of some peasants who lived on her husband's land in Platon-Café. The peasants were glad to see her and offered fresh vegetables and fruit for her to bring home.

As evening fell, the family gathered in the house and the storytelling began. Among the group was Madame Arbelle, a young, very dark, very beautiful woman, who was nursing her infant as the stories were being told.

At a pause she said, "I have a story. *Cric?*"

"*Crac!*" the others agreed. "She tells stories very well."

Madame Arbelle passed her infant to one of the relatives and told "Cat's Baptism." Each time she sang the meow, in a nasal tone, everyone would howl with laughter, and she would smile. But when she came to the end, "meow meow meow," then all the adults and children in the room joined her "meow meow meow meow" and she, laughing, opened her arms and took back her child.

IT was time for the smallest cat's baptism. Mr. and Mrs. Cat spoke with the child's godfather. They spoke with their relatives, and they spoke with the priest. The baptism was arranged for the following Sunday.

The Cat family, in their finest clothes, walked solemnly and proudly to the church. They sat in the front rows, attentive and eager. When the priest, a large brown cat, stepped onto the pulpit, the service began.

The priest sang:

> Meow meow meow
> meow meow.

All the members of the church responded:

> Meow meow meow
> meow meow.

The priest continued to chant:

> Meow meow meow
> meow meow.

And the congregation responded:

> Meow meow meow
> meow meow.

Then the priest held up his hand for silence and motioned to the godfather to step forward. "Please," the priest said, "kindly sing the prayers for your godchild."

The godfather sang:

> Meow

"I beg your pardon," the priest said. "I do not understand you. What was that?"

The godfather sang again:

Meow

"What?" the priest cried. "You are not singing properly at all. Sing after me."

Meow meow meow
meow.

The godfather sang:

Meow

"You are insulting the priest!" one of the cats from the other side of the church cried out, and he ran over and smacked the godfather. *YAOH!* Two members of the cat family rushed up and smacked him. *YAOH! Meow! PAAA!* One of the cats had bitten the tail of the priest, thinking he was the godfather. Five more cats joined the fight and soon all the cats in the church were fighting:

MEOW meow meow MEOW MEOW meow meow meow MEOW meow meow meow meow MEOW meow MEOW meow meow MEOW meow MEOW meow meow MEOW meow meow meow MEOW . . . . meow.

"I'm Tipingee,
She's Tipingee,
We're Tipingee, Too"

"I'm Tipingee,
She's Tipingee,
We're Tipingee, Too"

About the Story: Odette and I had driven to Croix-des-Missions to speak with André Pierre about painting the jacket of the book. Thirty years ago, André Pierre was a farmer with a very large family, none of whom had enough to eat. He was a *hungan* for his own family and had a special talent for painting the bowls and calabashes that were used in Voodoo ceremonies. Odette convinced him that it would not be sacrilegious to paint the same Voodoo decorations onto scratchboards and sell them. When Odette's friends saw the painting of Erzulie Fréda, Voodoo goddess of love, that André Pierre had painted for her, they immediately commissioned him to paint for them. Now, at seventy, André Pierre is one of the most revered and respected Haitian painters.

When we walked into his tiny studio, he was working on a painting of Baron-Samedi (General Death). It was twilight, and he continued to paint as we talked. We spoke about the folktales, and he said each had deep meaning. I mentioned the story of the magic orange tree. "That story I knew when I was a boy," he said. "Life from death—that is the orange tree. As we get closer to death, we understand more deeply the stories. The secrets of life are in the stories." I then asked him if he would paint a scene from the story of the orange tree to be used for the jacket of the folktale book. He was willing, but his price was beyond what I could afford.

We went back to speaking about the stories. It was nearly dark. André Pierre switched on one glaring electric light bulb, which hung from the ceiling. He offered us some kola and sent one of his grandsons (he proudly informed us he had over fifty) to gather together storytellers in the neighborhood for an evening's storytelling.

I had no painting for the jacket, but I was glad to have found another soul, a Haitian and a *hungan*, who also loved the orange tree story. And then later, in André Pierre's *houmfort*,* I heard Antoine Coleau tell in a simple, straightforward manner the story of Tipingee.

Two days afterwards, I went into Georges Nader's Gallery in Port-au-Prince. Lying on the floor against the door of his office was the painting I had asked André Pierre for—the painting of the magic orange tree. Where was Mr. Nader? He was there. And no, the painting had not been sold. And yes, I could buy it. And yes, I could afford it. It was by a young, unknown Haitian painter, who had just begun to paint, D. M. Maurice.

As I anxiously waited for it to be wrapped, a woman came over to me and offered me twice the price I had paid. I looked at her, amazed. *Sell* the painting of the magic orange tree? The moment the string was tied I was out of the store. I hid the painting under my bed until I left Haiti. I carried it onto the plane and into my editor's office in New York City. And when I took off the wrapping, she said: "The magic orange tree!"

* *houmfort*—Voodoo sanctuary

THERE was once a girl named Tipingee*
who lived with her stepmother. Her fa-
ther was dead. The stepmother was selfish, and even though she lived
in the girl's house she did not like to share what she earned with the
girl.

One morning, the stepmother was cooking sweets to sell in the
market. The fire under her pot went out. Tipingee was in school, so
the stepmother had to go herself into the forest to find more firewood.
She walked for a long time, but she did not find any wood. She continued walking. Then she came to a place where there was firewood
everywhere. She gathered it into a bundle. But it was too heavy to lift
up onto her head. Still, she did not want anyone else to have any of the
firewood. So standing in the middle of the forest she cried out: "My
friends, there is so much wood here and at home I have no wood.
Where can I find a person who will help me carry the firewood?"

Suddenly an old man appeared. "I will help you to carry the firewood. But then what will you give me?"

"I have very little," the woman said, "but I will find something
to give you when we get to my house."

The old man carried the firewood for the stepmother, and when
they got to the house he said, "I have carried the firewood for you.
Now what will you give me?"

"I will give you a servant girl. I will give you my stepdaughter,
Tipingee."

Now Tipingee was in the house, and when she heard her name
she ran to the door and listened.

"Tomorrow I will send my stepdaughter to the well at noon for
water. She will be wearing a red dress, call her by her name, Tipingee,
and she will come to you. Then you can take her."

"Very well," said the man, and he went away.

Tipingee ran to her friends. She ran to the houses of all the girls
in her class and asked them to wear red dresses the next day.

* Tipingee (Te-píng-gee): the "g" in the last syllable is pronounced as a hard "g"
as in "geese."

At noon the next day the old man went to the well. He saw one little girl dressed in red. He saw a second little girl dressed in red. He saw a third girl in red.

"Which of you is Tipingee?" he asked.

The first little girl said: "I'm Tipingee."

The second little girl said: "She's Tipingee."

The third little girl said: "We're Tipingee, too."

"Which of you is Tipingee?" asked the old man.

Then the little girls began to clap and jump up and down and chant:

> I'm Tipingee,
> She's Tipingee,
> We're Tipingee, too.
>
> I'm Tipingee,
> She's Tipingee,
> We're Tipingee, too.

Rah! The old man went to the woman and said, "You tricked me. All the girls were dressed in red and each one said she was Tipingee."

"That is impossible," said the stepmother. "Tomorrow she will wear a black dress. Then you will find her. The one wearing a black dress will be Tipingee. Call her and take her."

But Tipingee heard what her stepmother said and ran and begged all her friends to wear black dresses the next day.

When the old man went to the well the next day, he saw one little girl dressed in black. He saw a second little girl dressed in black. He saw a third girl in black.

"Which of you is Tipingee?" he asked.

The first little girl said: "I'm Tipingee."

The second little girl said: "She's Tipingee."

The third little girl said: "We're Tipingee, too."

"Which of you is Tipingee?" asked the old man.

And the girls joined hands and skipped about and sang:

I'm Tipingee,
She's Tipingee,
We're Tipingee, too.

I'm Tipingee,
She's Tipingee,
We're Tipingee, too.

The man was getting angry. He went to the stepmother and said, "You promised to pay me and you are only giving me problems. You tell me Tipingee and everyone here is Tipingee, Tipingee, Tipingee, Tipingee. If this happens a third time, I will come and take you for my servant."

"My dear sir," said the stepmother, "tomorrow she will be in red, completely in red, call her and take her."

And again Tipingee ran and told her friends to dress in red.

At noon the next day, the old man arrived at the well. He saw one little girl dressed in red. He saw a second little girl dressed in red. He saw a third girl in red.

"Which of you is Tipingee?" he asked.

"I'm Tipingee," said the first girl.

"She's Tipingee," said the second girl.

"We're Tipingee, too," said the third girl.

"WHICH OF YOU IS TIPINGEE?" the old man shouted.

But the girls just clapped and jumped up and down and sang:

I'm Tipingee,
She's Tipingee,
We're Tipingee, too.

I'm Tipingee,
She's Tipingee,
We're Tipingee, too.

The old man knew he would never find Tipingee. He went to the stepmother and took her away. When Tipingee returned home, she was gone. So she lived in her own house with all her father's belongings, and she was happy.

The Master Thief

The Master Thief

About the Story: Willy told this story on my first visit to Dr. Philippe's house. On my next visit I asked him to tell it again. He did so almost verbatim. He loved all the trickery. When he said, "Why he did not take his goat and boot with him, I do not know," both times he doubled up laughing.

I had asked him to tell it again because the ending seemed somewhat abrupt, but he ended it the same way. I asked Jeanne Philippe about the tale and she said it was a very old one and that she had heard it when she was young. Even then, she said, there was mention of the bank and electricity, and it ended in the same way.

THERE was a wealthy man who had three sons. He paid for their education, and they were good students. After they had finished their schooling, he asked them what trade they wanted to follow.

"Papa, I want to be a lawyer," said the first one.

"That is fine," the father said. So the boy packed his bags and the father sent him to law school.

"Papa, I want to be a tailor," said the second.

"That is also fine," the father said. The boy packed his bags and the father apprenticed him to a master tailor.

"Papa, I would like to be a thief," said the third son.

"I do not think I heard you correctly."

"You heard me correctly, Papa. I want to study to be a master thief."

"How can this be? I spend my money to educate you, and deprive myself, and all you want is to steal. Why don't you choose something useful like your other two brothers?"

"But, Papa, one can only work according to one's abilities. Please, Papa, apprentice me to the shoemaker, the Boss shoemaker in the village who is known for his tricks."

So the father took his son to the Boss shoemaker. "Teach him what you can," he said.

The shoemaker was rather surprised that the son of such a wealthy man wanted to work for him, but he soon saw that the boy was earnest.

In a very short time the boy became adept at explaining to the customers: "Not ready yet. Oh, come back tomorrow." "Did I say Friday? I meant the following Friday." "Really, you must be patient."

Many of the customers became so tired of waiting for their old shoes to be repaired that they bought new ones. So the shoemaker sold the old ones and by this and other tricks he made a tidy profit.

But one evening, the shoemaker and his student were sitting by the public road and the shoemaker was cooking rice. It seemed that his customers had been unusually patient lately so he was unable to buy meat. They were forced to eat dry rice without any sauce.

"We never ate like this at home," the boy said. "We had meat at both lunch and dinner, and bananas and potatoes as well."

"In my profession one must show patience when one's customers are patient," the shoemaker replied.

"Even so," the boy said.

Then they noticed a peasant in the distance leading his goat toward them on his way to market.

"You see that goat?" the boy said. "We are eating goat tonight."

"But how?"

"Give me one of your better boots and go hide in the bushes."

The boy took the boot and laid it in the road so the peasant would be sure to see it as he passed. The peasant walked by with his goat, noticed the boot, but did not stop. The boy then snatched up the boot, raced through the bushes, and laid it in the road in front of the peasant. As the man approached the boot he slowed down.

"Awhile back I saw one boot," he said to himself. "This makes two. If I had them both I would have a pair."

So the man tied his goat to a mapou tree and went back for the first boot. Why he did not take his goat and the boot with him, I do not know. Well, the boy quickly untied the goat and led him to the Boss shoemaker. They feasted on goat meat for several days, and the Boss was pleased.

A week later they happened to be sitting in the same place by the public road and saw the same peasant walking toward them leading another goat.

"We shall eat goat meat again," the boy said.

"But how? You don't think you can fool the same man twice do you?"

"Wait and see."

The boy rushed ahead of the peasant and waited for him in the bushes by the mapou tree. As the peasant approached, he began to bray: *"Be-be Be-be Be-be."* The peasant stopped to listen. The boy brayed louder to excite him. *"BE-BE BE-BE BE-BE BE-BE."*

"That must be my lost goat, calling me," the man said. He tied his goat to the mapou tree and started into the bushes.

The boy continued braying for a time, leading the man farther and farther from the road. Then he doubled back, untied the goat, and quickly led him to the Boss shoemaker.

When the man could not find his goat and came back to the road and found his other goat was gone, he said, "It's this tree. There is a spirit in this tree that is making my goats invisible."

"You are doing very well," the Boss said to the boy. "I think you will be getting your diploma soon."

"That is good. I am ready to begin working seriously."

The following week the shoemaker said, "Here is one gourde. Take it to market and buy me beans, rice, spices, and whee-ai. If you can buy all of that with one gourde, I will give you your diploma."

The boy paid fifteen centimes for beans, rice, and spices. He had

138

five centimes left to buy whee-ai. But he didn't know what whee-ai was. He asked at all the stalls, but no one had any whee-ai. "I will tell him there is no whee-ai at the market this week," he thought and with the five centimes he bought himself some candy.

Near the gate of the shoemaker's house was a chadèque* tree. As the boy passed it he remembered how hot and peppery the pits of its fruit were. So he picked one fruit, opened it, and put the pits in his pocket. Then he went around to the back and handed the Boss shoemaker the groceries, but as he did so, he acted startled. "Oh-oh," he said. "You look terrible. Are you sick? Quick, put out your tongue."

Without thinking, the Boss opened his mouth and the boy threw the pits onto the Boss's tongue. "*Wheee-Allll!*" the Boss shouted.

"Now I have given you all you asked," the boy said, "and I would like my diploma."

"With pleasure!" the Boss shoemaker answered, "I am afraid to work under the same roof with you. You are too skillful for me."

With his diploma in his hand, the boy walked home. He was proud of his diploma but wise enough to know that his parents might not be glad to see either him or his diploma. His father owned a very large estate with land that stretched for kilometers. On the edge of his father's land, the boy built himself a rough shack. Then he began to work seriously. After working steadily for many months, he had enough money to build a beautiful house.

One day, the father was walking on his property and saw a house larger and more beautiful than his own. He wondered who would dare to build on his land and he knocked on the door.

"Papa!" the young man said. "Come in." He welcomed his father and showed him his house—his new furniture, his paintings, his rugs, and his sacks filled with gold and silver coins.

"Why haven't you been to see us?" the father asked.

"I have been working very seriously, and I was not certain you would approve of my kind of work."

"Work is good," the father answered. "Only I am surprised that you who have so much seem to have forgotten us."

* chadèque (pronounced "shadek") is a kind of grapefruit.

"Oh, no," the son said, and he offered his father a sack filled with money.

The father accepted it and soon left.

Several days later the father returned, and his son offered him another sack of money. When the father came for a third visit and the son handed him still another sack, he paused.

"Tell me," the father asked, "how is it that you have given me so much money and yet your supply seems to remain the same? You have as many sacks today as you had on my first visit."

"I work steadily, Papa. I practice my profession conscientiously."

"Your profession interests me. Do you think I am too old to learn?"

"In my profession it is not age but skill that counts."

"Well?"

"Well, if you like, come to my house this evening in a dark suit and bring an empty sack, and you'll see."

The two men walked that evening to the village.

"We are going in here," the son said, stopping before a bank. When they were inside, the son said, "Stand by the door, Papa, and don't move. Don't move and don't touch anything. I'm going to fill up our bags."

While the father was standing there, he noticed something on the wall that interested him. He put out his hand and touched it, but it was live electricity. *Yow.* He fell to the floor dead.

The son ran over to his father, but the father was quite dead. He tried to pick him up. The body was big and heavy. "What am I going to do?" the son thought. "If I leave him here, he'll be found and they'll come to question Mama and me. If I try to take him home, I'll be caught."

The master thief took out his knife and cut off his father's head. He put it in one of the sacks, and went to his mother's house.

When the bank was opened the next day, the body was found. And just as the master thief had presupposed, the police took the body and began to make an inquiry in the neighborhood. The young man did not leave his mother's side.

"Who has lost someone? Who has lost someone?" the police chanted, as they came up the road toward the mother's house.

The son ran to his mother and put a sharp knife and a stick of sugar cane in her hand. "Peel the sugar cane," he told her.

Then, as the police entered with his father's body and the mother cried "Oh," the master thief pushed his mother's hand against the knife. "Oh, Mama, look, you have cut yourself with the knife and are bleeding."

"Oh!!!" The mother fainted.

"Oh, Mama," he said bending over her and slapping her face. Then he turned to the police and explained. "She's so sensitive, just one drop of blood and she faints. She's always been this way. We have to be so careful—"

And the police, not wanting to bother with such a family, turned and left the house, chanting, "Who has lost someone? Who has lost someone?"

So it was that the master thief saved the family's honor. Some time later he buried the head, and no one ever found out the identity of the decapitated corpse.

Horse and
Toad

Horse and Toad

About the Story: Elmir Innocent, a young woman of twenty, told the story of Horse and Toad's race in a clear, engaging, dramatic manner at Masson. When she sang Toad's song, she provocatively moved her hips from side to side. When she sang Horse's song, she hardly moved, holding her head in the air. The audience joined her full-heartedly. I, too, was singing Toad's song along with everyone. When Elmir finished, I suddenly jumped up and shouted: *"Cric?"* There was a loud and astonished *"CRAC!"* from the audience.

This was my third trip to Haiti and my fifth visit to Masson. For a long time, I'd been wanting to share with the Haitian storytellers some of the stories I knew. I'd been wanting—but waiting. Now as I stood there ready to begin, I realized why I had been right in waiting. In Masson, any storyteller who received a *crac!* started off at a lively trot, whereas my Creole still only moved word by word. But here in Masson the heat and fire and spark of storytelling caught me.

I began with the Russian tale of an old man and woman who had a bet as to which could remain silent the longest. They both became ill, and when at last the mayor (I used *hungan*) came into their house and offered the old woman's coat to anyone

144

who would take care of the silent couple, the woman jumped up and shouted: "What? Not *my* new coat!"

I used more pantomime than words and strode and jumped and leaped about the dirt area where the storytellers performed. I made great arm movements and lots of grimaces. I saw each child's and each adult's wide-eyed expression as I moved from person to person. Do they understand? Do they understand? was all that went through my mind.

The children were laughing—what a marvel to see a white woman in glasses and blue jeans (Haitian peasant women always wear dresses) and a funny accent making such faces. The adults were laughing and also watching intently. In the end everyone laughed and clapped. I sat down shaking and sweating, my heart thumping.

For several moments I could neither see nor hear. Then, somewhere in the outer periphery: "*Li conté bien.*" And another voice: "*Li conté bien.*" "She tells stories well," they were saying. I closed my eyes . . . overcome.

THE king of Léogane* had three daughters. The first two were quickly married, but it took a long time for someone to come for the third. Then suddenly, on the same day, two suitors appeared before the king and asked to marry his daughter. The two suitors were Horse and Toad.

Of course the king preferred to have Horse as his son-in-law, for Horse would be much more useful, but he pretended to be fair, so he said, "My dear sirs, since I have only one daughter and since there are two of you who love her, the only fair way to decide between you

* Léogane is pronounced "Lay-o-gahn." There was never a king of Léogane, but during the French occupation, Léogane and Cap-Haitien were the two seats of government. The only king of Haiti was Jean-Christophe. Before him, the French plantation owners governed their regions by appointment of the French Crown.

is to hold a contest. I will ask both of you to run a race from Brâche*
to Léogane this Sunday. The one who arrives first will marry the
princess.

When Horse heard the terms of the contest, he was delighted. He
was certain he would win, for no one could run faster than he. But
Toad had his ideas, too.

On Sunday, the princess was seated in a comfortable straw chair
in Léogane, surrounded by friends and relatives. Horse and Toad
waited side by side in the road at Brâche.

The king's representatives cried out: "Go!"

The race was on. But neither Horse nor Toad moved.

"Please take the lead," Horse said gallantly. "We both know that
I can run faster than you."

"No, no," said Toad cordially, "*you* take the lead, for I shall
win."

Horse and Toad stood arguing in the middle of the road, each
gesturing for the other to go first.

"You," said Horse.

"No, no, please," said Toad.

Finally the king's representatives came up and gave them both a
good kick in the behind. "Now—go!" they cried, "and don't forget
to stop and sing at each signpost."

Horse and Toad were off. Horse quickly gained the lead and
trotted along at an easy pace. When he reached the first signpost he
sang slowly and pompously:**

> Ekoray, Samba!
> Ekoray, Samba!
> Ekoray, Samba!
> Ekoray, Samba!

He was about to start off for the next signpost when he heard
Toad begin his song:***

* Brâche (pronounced "Brahsh") is three miles from Léogane. A rich sugar-pro-
ducing area, it was named after De Brache, the devious, strong-minded French
lieutenant-governor of the Léogane region (1710–60).
** See music p. 206.
*** See music p. 207.

Tell me,
Tell me, tell me, tell me
O tell me true.
How can a tiny little toad
Like me
Win
A lovely girl like you?

Horse was amazed, for he was certain he had left Toad far behind. Horse now trotted faster. When he reached the second signpost he began his song immediately:

Ekoray, Samba!
Ekoray, Samba!
Ekoray, Sam-

But before Horse had finished his song, Toad began his song:

Tell me,
Tell me, tell me, tell me
O tell me true.
How can a tiny little toad
Like me
Win
A lovely girl like you?

Now Horse ran fast. Fast, fast, fast, fast, fast. He was running and he was sweating, but just as he got to the third signpost, he heard Toad singing:

Tell me,
Tell me, tell me, tell me
O tell me true.
How can a tiny little toad
Like me
Win
A lovely girl like you?

How was it possible? Horse looked around for the tiny slimy creature so he could trample him and go on to win the race himself. But Toad darted under some straw at the side of the road.

"Sing!" the king's representatives at the third signpost ordered. Horse sang his song:

> Ekoray Samba.
> Ekoray Samba.
> Ekoray Samba.
> Ekoray Samba.

Then Horse ran. He ran and ran and ran and ran and ran and ran and ran and ran. But it was no use. No matter how fast Horse might run, Toad was already there. The other toads along the road were four of Toad's relatives. The real Toad, the princess's suitor, was sitting all this time under her chair waiting. And as soon as the real Toad saw the dust rising up in the road and Horse racing toward them, he leaped into her lap and sang:

> Tell me
> Tell me, tell me, tell me
> O tell me true.
> How can a tiny little toad
> Like me
> Win
> A lovely girl like you?

The princess tried to push Toad away, but he clung to her skirt. Then Horse came rushing up, but the people said: "Too late. Toad is the victor."

So even though the king had wanted Horse to win, and had purposely arranged the terms of the contest so that Horse *could* win, Toad was more clever. And it was Toad who won the contest and married the princess.

Mother
of the
Waters

Mother
of the
Waters

About the Story: Whenever I have told this story I have been questioned as to whether this is an authentic folktale. Listeners are puzzled by the idea of a young girl disobeying the magic figure of the Mother of the Waters. It is rather daring for an inexperienced person to go against the magic of a spirit.

Though the act of disobedience is unusual in folktales, this particular story was recorded by Suzanne Comhaire-Sylvain in Haiti, and the version she published in 1937 is nearly identical to the one I recorded in Haiti in 1973. In her version, the girl articulates her thoughts and says, "I can not obey the old woman, that cat is hungry."

It may be that Comhaire-Sylvain was also intrigued by the question of disobedience, for she chose to write the first part of her doctoral thesis (*Les Contes Haitiens*) at the Sorbonne on just this story. In her thesis, Comhaire-Sylvain describes over one hundred parallel versions of "Mother of the Waters." The ones that most closely resemble the Haitian one are from the Caribbean (they contain the search for water, the old woman with sores, the cooking, the large and small eggs, and the beating of the cat) and from Africa (the same images, but no beating of the cat). The images of fertility are different in both the American Indian (Spiderwoman, large and small pottery jugs) and the European (the oven, the cow, the feather bed, the apple tree). But in all these versions there are only six in which there is any act of disobedience.

A young seamstress told this story one evening after work as she was sitting with her co-workers in a tiny dress shop in Pétionville. She was timid and correct in her behavior toward her boss, but once she began the story, she was in her own world. She spoke quietly and intently, as if she were seeing each image as she spoke it.

THERE was once a young girl whose mother and father were both dead. As she had no way to get anything to eat, she had to hire herself out as a servant. She worked for a woman who lived by the river. But even though the woman had a daughter the same age as the servant girl, she showed no kindness to her. She beat her and spoke roughly to her and gave her only scraps to eat.

One day, the woman sent the servant girl to the river to wash the silverware. As the girl was washing the silver, a tiny silver teaspoon slipped through her fingers and was carried away by the water. The servant girl reached for the teaspoon, but the current was moving too swiftly. She went back to the house and told her mistress what had happened.

"Find my teaspoon," the woman screamed, "or never return to my house."

The servant girl returned to the river and followed the stream. She walked all day without finding the teaspoon, and as the sun began to set in the sky, she started crying.

An old woman sitting on a stone near the river's edge asked her why she was crying.

"I have dropped my mistress's silver teaspoon in the river. She says if I do not find it, I may not return. I will have no work. How will I eat?"

The old woman did not answer. Instead, she asked, "Will you wash my back?"

"Of course," the girl answered.

She soaped and scrubbed the old woman's back, but the woman's back was rough and hard and covered with sores and thistles, and the girl's hands were soon bleeding.

"What is it?" the woman asked.

"It is nothing," the girl answered.

"Let me see your hands," the old woman said.

The girl held them out. The old woman spit on them. The cuts closed up and the girl's hands were as they were before.

"Come home with me," the old woman said, "and I will give you dinner."

She led the girl to her home in the mountains and gave her banana pudding. Then they went to sleep.

The next day, after the girl had swept the yard, the woman gave her a bone, a grain of rice, and one bean and told her to make dinner.

"Grandmother," the girl said respectfully, "please forgive me, but I do not know how to make dinner with these."

"It is simple," the old woman said. "Place them in a pot of boiling water and dinner will soon be ready."

The girl followed the woman's directions, and by noon a delicious-smelling casserole of rice, beans, and meat was steaming inside the pot.

As they ate the old woman told the girl: "I will be going out. In a few hours a wild cat will come and beg for food. Do not give it any food. Beat it with my stick."

A few hours after the old woman left, the girl heard a mewing outside the door. *Me-ow. Me-ow. Me-ow.* The cat was so thin and hungry the girl did not have the heart to hit it. She brought it a saucer of milk and watched it eat. After a while the cat went away.

A short time later the old woman returned. She was pleased with the girl. So the servant girl stayed on with the old woman. The girl helped her, and the old woman always gave her enough to eat.

Then, after several months, the old woman told her it was time for her to return to her mistress.

"Yes," said the girl. "But how can I go back without the silver teaspoon?"

"Walk down the road," the old woman said. "When you come to the first crossroads you will see a pile of eggs lying on some straw. The larger ones will call out: *Take me, take me!* Take one of the smaller eggs and break it open at the next crossroads."

The servant girl thanked the old woman and set out.

At the first crossroads she saw the pile of eggs. The larger ones cried: *Take me, take me!* The girl chose the smallest egg and when she cracked it open at the next crossroads, out came a tiny box, which grew and grew until it filled her arms. The girl opened it and inside were forks and knives and spoons—all made of silver.

The woman and her daughter were so jealous when they saw the servant girl's box of silverware that they made her tell the story of how she had gotten it three times. Then the very next morning, the mother sent her own daughter down to the river to wash the silverware.

The girl didn't even bother to wash the silverware. She simply threw the small coffee teaspoon into the river and went home.

"I have lost the coffee spoon," the girl declared.

"Then go and find it," the mother said knowingly, "and do not come home until you do."

The daughter walked alongside the river all day. Then, toward evening, she saw the old woman sitting on a stone. Immediately she began to cry.

"Why are you crying?" the woman asked.

"Oh-oh. I have lost my mother's silver spoon. She says I may not go home unless I find it. What shall I do?"

"Will you wash my back?" the woman asked.

The girl took the soap and began to wash the woman's back when the thistles on the woman's back cut her hands.

"Oh-oh!" she cried.

"What is it?" asked the woman.

"It's your filthy rotting back. It cut my hands and they are bleeding."

The old woman took the girl's hands and spit on them and they were healed. Then she brought her to her home in the mountains and fed her supper.

The next morning, the old woman gave the girl a bone, a grain of rice, and one bean and told her to make dinner.

"With this garbage?" said the girl.

"What a sorry tongue you have," the woman answered. "I only hope you are not as nasty as your words. Place what I have given you in a pot of boiling water and dinner will soon be ready."

At noon the pot was filled with rice and beans and meat. They ate their meal and the old woman said:

"I am going out. In a few hours a wild cat will come and beg for food. Do not give it any food. Beat it with my stick."

Some time after the old woman left, the girl heard a mewing outside. *Me-ow. Me-ow. Me-ow.* She grabbed the old woman's stick and rushed for the cat. She hit it and hit it and hit it and hit it until she broke one of its legs.

Much later that evening, the old woman returned. She was leaning on a cane and limping, for one of her legs was broken. The next morning she told the girl: "You must leave my house today. You will not learn and I cannot help you anymore."

"But I will not go home without my silverware," the girl insisted.

"Then I shall give you one last bit of advice. At the next crossroads you will find a pile of eggs lying on some straw. The larger ones will call out: *Take me, take me!* Choose one of the smaller eggs and break it open at the next crossroads."

The girl ran out of the house and down the road. When she came to the first crossroads the larger eggs called out: *Take me, take me!*

"I am not foolish," said the girl. "If an egg speaks to me, I will listen. If it is a large one, all the better!"

She chose the largest egg and broke it open at the next crossroads. Out came all kinds of lizards, goblins, demons, and devils and ate the girl up.

A Very
Happy Donkey

A Very
Happy Donkey

About the Story: Elsie, a seamstress of about six-
teen years old, told this story at Jeanne Philippe's.
She told it in a quiet, amused manner, only raising
her voice for the donkey's loud cries, *HEE-huh*,
and at the end when Tiroro calls for help.

When Tiroro was desperate, he called on the
Haitian peasant trinity: Jesus Christ, Damballah
Oueddo, and Papa God. Tiroro was probably bap-
tized and maybe even received communion (most
peasants attend the Catholic Church for baptisms
and funerals and, when they can afford it, for com-
munions and weddings). It is possible that Damballah Oueddo, who is at the head of the Haitian
spirits, was also Tiroro's own ancestral spirit. Yet
of the three called upon, it is Papa God who responds to Tiroro. With his movable domain and his
flexible schedule, Papa God happened to be in the
vicinity at the moment of Tiroro's plea.

There was much joking in the audience when
Elsie described Tiroro as a wastrel, vagabond,
and drummer. The storytellers that evening were
young, many of them under twenty, and all of
them (with the exception of Willy) were already
working. They enjoyed hearing about Tiroro's
blissful state of laziness. They knew too well how
soon it would be over.

158

THERE was once a woman named Tiyaya and she had a son named Tiroro and a donkey named Banda. She lived in the mountains in a small hut with one door, one window, one table, one chair, and one mat. Her only son, Tiroro, was a wastrel and a vagabond. He never helped his mother, even with the gardening, but spent his days and nights playing the drum.

One morning Tiyaya woke up and she was sick. "Tiroro, I am so tired I cannot move. You must go to market for me today. Eat your breakfast and go saddle Banda."

Tiroro finished his breakfast of maïs moulu* and went to find Banda. Banda was nibbling grass under a tree.

"Come now, Banda," Tiroro said.

"*HEE-huh*. Where are we going?" Banda asked.

"To market," Tiroro answered, leading her back to the house.

Then he saddled Banda and tied two large baskets to the saddle. One he filled with fresh carrots and the other with fresh turnips and cauliflower.

"Tiroro," his mother called to him from the house.

"Yes, Mama."

"Have you the carrots?"

"Yes, Mama."

"And the turnips?"

"Yes, Mama."

"And the cauliflower?"

"Yes, Mama. I've everything. Everything. We're leaving now, Mama."

"And Banda, did you take food for Banda?"

"Yes, Mama. I've everything."

"Then may Papa God go with you. . . . And get a good price for the vegetables."

Tiroro and Banda walked along the mountain path and soon came across other peasants on their way to market. As they walked they told stories and sang and joked and the time went by quickly.

* Maïs ("Mye-is") moulu is ground corn that is cooked similarly to rice.

When they reached Pétionville the sun was setting. The others stopped to rest for a few hours. Tiroro decided to do the same. The others unsaddled their donkeys. Tiroro unsaddled Banda. He brought her water in a pail and tied her rope to a stake in the earth. Then he ate a few carrots and lay down to sleep with his head on the baskets.

It seemed to Tiroro that he had just closed his eyes when he heard Banda braying: "*HEE-huh! HEE-huh! HEE-huh!*"

"What is it, Banda?" Tiroro whispered. "Are you hungry?" He reached his hand into the basket and took out two cauliflowers and brought them to Banda. Banda munched peacefully on the cauliflowers and Tiroro lay down again.

A half hour passed, then: "*HEE-huh! HEE-huh!*"

"Again!" Tiroro said, waking up. "You're still hungry?" He reached into the basket and brought out a bundle of turnips and walked over to Banda. Banda munched on the turnips and Tiroro lay down.

But ten minutes later: "*HEE-huh! HEE-huh!*"

"Banda, let me sleep!"

"*HEE-huh! HEE-huh! HEE-huh! HEE-huh!*"

"Carrots! Maybe that's what you want!" Tiroro said. And he took two bundles of carrots from the other basket and brought them to Banda. But now that Banda had tasted all the vegetables she was hungrier than ever:

"*HEE-huh! HEE-huh! HEE-huh! HEE-huh! HEE-huh!*"

Banda brayed so loudly the man sleeping next to Tiroro shouted: "Shut that donkey up!"

"What shall I do with you?" Tiroro cried. He was so sleepy and tired. In desperation he went and brought both baskets of vegetables and placed them by the stake in front of Banda. "Now eat and let me sleep!" he said.

A few hours later Tiroro woke up. The peasants were saddling their donkeys. Tiroro saddled Banda. He picked up the baskets. Oh-oh. ... Oh-oh. The baskets were empty. There was nothing in them. Banda had eaten every carrot, every turnip, and every bit of cauliflower during the night.

The son of Tiyaya burst into tears. "In the name of Papa God, in

Elsa Henriquez

the name of Our Lord Jesus Christ, in the name of Damballah Oueddo,* what shall I do? Someone answer me! What shall I do?

Papa God answered Tiroro. He said: *"Next time feed your donkey grass."*

Poor Tiroro. He cried and cried. The others continued on their way to market. What was Tiroro to do? He turned up the mountain path toward his home, with an empty stomach, two empty baskets, and a *very* happy donkey.

"HEE-huh! HEE-huh! HEE-huh!"

Banda!

---

* Damballah Oueddo is pronounced "Dam-bal-lah Way-do."

"One, My Darling,
Come to Mama"

"One, My Darling, Come to Mama"

About the Story: Pradel Parent, who was my chief translator, grew up in the countryside near Mayanman and led the rural life of a peasant. He had obviously heard many stories when he was young, for when he would listen to the stories on tape, after a few minutes he would nod his head and laugh and say, "Yes-yes." It seemed to me he knew a good third of the stories I had recorded. Sometimes he would say, "Yes, that's the way it goes, that's the one I know." Other times he would say, "No, he is telling it differently."

Most Haitian peasants do not speak or understand French. Pradel was bilingual because he had learned French from his father, who was a schoolteacher in the mountains. Pradel knew no English. He worked as a manager in a cassette factory in Port-au-Prince and after work would come to the Sans-Souci Hotel to help me translate the stories from Creole to French. Sometimes he also accompanied me at night to the storytellings.

He was responsible and efficient and always eager to work and to please. But he had a certain melancholy about him. He often spoke bitterly about his father because his father had gone off with another woman and abandoned his mother and himself and his sister, Marie. One evening when we were talking, he said: "Now *I* will tell you a story." It was the only folktale he told me: "One, My Darling, Come to Mama."

THERE was once a woman who had four daughters. She loved the first three and despised the fourth. Each time she brought food home for her children, she would stand outside the door and sing:*

One, my darling, come to Mama,
Two, my darling, come to Mama,
Three, my darling, come to Mama,
Stay, Philamandré, stay,
Stay where you are.

The older daughters would run to the door and let their mother in. Philamandré remained in the corner. The three girls and their mother would sit at the table and eat. And if there was any food left, it would be given to Philamandré. The three older girls grew fat and sleek. Philamandré was thin as a nail.

Now a devil had been watching the mother for a long time. He saw how the mother would arrive at her house and sing, and how the young girls would run to the door. He had secretly been practicing her song:

One, my darling, come to Mama,
Two, my darling, come to Mama,
Three, my darling, come to Mama,
Stay, Philamandré, stay,
Stay where you are.

At last the devil decided he was ready. He came to the door and sang in a deep gruff voice:

* See music p. 208.

167

One, my darling, come to Mama,
Two, my darling, come to Mama,
Three, my darling, come to Mama,
Stay, Philamandré, stay,
Stay where you are.

But, of course, the girls knew the gruff voice was not their mother's and did not open the door. The devil went to see the plumber.

"Tighten my voice," he said. "Tighten it as much as you can, so it will be as high as possible."

When the devil returned to the house of the young girls, his voice was three octaves higher and sounded like a bird:

One, my darling, come to Mama,
Two, my darling, come to Mama,
Three, my darling, come to Mama,
Stay, Philamandré, stay,
Stay where you are.

"Some silly bird," the girls said to each other and did not go to the door.

A little later their mother returned and sang:

One, my darling, come to Mama,
Two, my darling, come to Mama,
Three, my darling, come to Mama,
Stay, Philamandré, stay,
Stay where you are.

The girls at once recognized her voice and let her in. As always the four ate together, leaving the scraps to Philamandré.

The devil went back to the plumber and complained, "You tightened it too much." So the plumber loosened it a bit and when the devil returned the next day, his voice sounded just like the mother's:

> One, my darling, come to Mama,
> Two, my darling, come to Mama,
> Three, my darling, come to Mama,
> Stay, Philamandré, stay,
> Stay where you are.

The girls ran to the door to let their mother in and the devil grabbed all three and ran off with them.

Philamandré remained in the corner.

After a while the mother returned and sang:

> One, my darling, come to Mama,
> Two, my darling, come to Mama,
> Three, my darling, come to Mama,
> Stay, Philamandré, stay,
> Stay where you are.

No one came to the door. The mother sang again:

> One, my darling, come to Mama,
> Two, my darling, come to Mama,
> Three, my darling, come to Mama,
> Stay, Philamandré, stay,
> Stay where you are.

Still no one came. Where were her dear ones? Then she heard:

> One cannot come to Mama,
> Two cannot come to Mama,
> Three cannot come to Mama,
> Philamandré is
> Where she is.

The mother pushed open the door and when she did not see anyone she ran from the house like a madwoman, singing her song to anyone who would listen.

Philamandré walked out the open door, down the road to town. She found work, and after some time, she married the king's son.

Many years later a madwoman was heard singing in the street:

> One cannot come to Mama,
> Two cannot come to Mama,
> Three cannot come to Mama,
> Philamandré is
> Where she is.

The king's servants tried to hurry her away from the palace. She was in rags, and her wild hair, filled with droppings of birds, looked like branches of a tree. But every day she would come back and sing:

> One cannot come to Mama,
> Two cannot come to Mama,
> Three cannot come to Mama,
> Philamandré is
> Where she is.

Then one day the queen's servant said to the queen, "There is a ragged woman in the street who calls every afternoon for Philamandré. Do you know anyone of that name?"

The queen rushed to the window. The woman in the street, the beggar woman, was her own mother. She went down and brought her into the palace. She washed her and gave her new clothes and cut her hair.

"Mama," she said, "the others are no more. But I am here. Look at me, I am Philamandré. You did not care for me, but I am here, and now I will take care of you."

The Forbidden Apple

The Forbidden Apple

About the Story: Antoine St. Louis, a farmer of about forty years, told this story at Carrefour-Dufort. He stood as he acted out the different characters, and when the sisters jumped over the hole, he did a sort of skipping dance. In this story the audience did not join him on the song; he sang by himself. His voice dramatically wailed, moaned, and sobbed as the sisters sang and cried to their father. The audience listened intently. When he delivered the last line, a man in the crowd called out: "That's right, that's true."

The majority of the stories I heard ended with formalized endings. The most frequent one was a version of: "I was passing by and saw them, but when they saw me, they kicked me so hard, that's how I got here today to tell you the story." I used this form once, to begin the book. There were two other approaches: Many of the best storytellers, instead of using conventional endings, would pause a moment, let the silence enter, and then cry: "End of story!" A third approach was for the storyteller to give his or her own commentary on the events. When Justine tried this at the end of "The Singing Bone," it was not accepted, but when Antoine did so at the end of "The Forbidden Apple," the audience was satisfied.

THERE was once a father who had three children, Bon Bazie, Mazalie, and a son named Léon. The two girls were obedient and well-behaved, but Léon was a gambler and spent his days playing cards and dice.

The sisters were afraid of their father. What he said he would do, he did, and when he was determined to do something, no one dared stand in his path. No one even tried. Not his daughters, nor his wife, who was long since dead, and certainly not his neighbors. There was no one, well yes, there was Léon . . . and Léon was always provoking his father.

One day the father came home at noon with a bright red apple in his hand. He placed it on the table and said, "This apple is for my dinner. If anyone eats it I will throw them in the hole in the garden and the earth over them."

Soon after the father left, Léon entered the house.

"Léon," his sisters said, "here are some rice and beans for dinner."

"Hmm, what a rosy apple," Léon said.

"Léon!" his sisters shouted. "Do not touch that apple—it is Papa's. He said if anyone ate it, he would—"

"Papa's apple, then of course I shall eat it. Why shouldn't I eat the apple? Shall I go next door and beg our neighbors for an apple?"

"Léon!" the girls implored.

"What is Papa's is mine." And Léon picked up the apple and bit into it. No one spoke. There was silence in the house as he ate it. Then he left.

When the father returned from work, his eyes went directly to the empty space on the table.

"Who has taken my apple?" he called.

No one answered.

"WHO HAS EATEN MY APPLE?" he shouted.

"Léon," the girls whispered.

"Go into the garden this minute," the father said. "Each of you will jump over the hole, over and over and over, until the one who took my apple admits to having done so."

Bon Bazie, Mazalie, and their father went into the garden. Léon had not come home yet.

As Bon Bazie jumped across the hole, she sang: *

> Papa, it's not me
> It's Léon.
> Nor is it Mazalie
> It's Léon.
> But even if he's the one,
> He's your only son.

Then it was Mazalie's turn and she sang:

> Papa, it's not me
> It's Léon.
> Nor is it Bon Bazie
> It's Léon.
> But even if he's the one,
> He's your only son.

"Léon!" the father shouted. But Léon had not come home yet. It was dark now.

"Go over the hole again," the father said. "Over and over and over."

Bon Bazie jumped across the hole. She was singing and she was crying:

> Papa, it's not me
> It's Léon.
> Nor is it Mazalie
> It's Léon.
> But even if he's the one,
> He's your only son.

Then Mazalie ran and she was crying as she sang, crying for her brother:

* See music p. 208–209.

> Papa, it's not me
> It's Léon.
> Nor is it Bon Bazie
> It's Léon.
> But even if he's the one,
> He's your only son.

"Léon!"
"Yes, Papa." Léon came out of the shadows.
"Léon," the father ordered. "Jump over the hole."
Léon jumped across and proudly and slowly sang:

> Papa, it is me.
> I am Léon.
> Papa, it is me.
> I am Léon.
> But even if I did so,
> Why should I not do so?

When the father heard that, he seized Léon and threw him into the hole, killing him. The father threw dirt over him and the sisters cried and cried, but that was the end of Léon.

Let me tell you something—that father was cruel, and that father was harsh, but that was his nature and Léon knew it. If ever I had a father like that, and he told me, "Don't touch my things!" I would never touch his things. Never.

"Papa God First,
Man Next,
Tiger Last"

"Papa God First, Man Next, Tiger Last"

About the Story: Luders, the storyteller, was a strong and handsome farm laborer from the Masson area. He did not move about as he spoke, but stood with his feet firmly planted on the ground about a foot and a half apart. He expressed himself with a vibrant voice and flashing eyes and teeth, making clear, decisive gestures. He had confidence and assurance and a certain sweetness.

As he spoke I thought to myself, here is a child deeply loved and cared for by his mother. Despite the preponderance of harsh "mothers" in the Haitian folktales, the children survive and a few even blossom. Luders' story is about a mother who refuses to sacrifice her child, regardless of who is to be called "first."

THERE is an old saying: "Papa God first, Man next, Tiger last."

One day Tiger* cornered Man by the water and asked him, "Is the old saying true: 'Papa God first, Man next, Tiger last'?"

---

* Tiger (*tigre*) is a generic term used in Haiti and the Caribbean since the seventeenth century for wild, ferocious animals of the cat family. There is no record of tigers having inhabited Haiti.

178

"If you will let me climb that coconut tree, I will tell you," Man said.

"Climb the tree," Tiger said.

Man climbed the tree. When he was high in the tree, far from the ground, he shouted: "It is true: 'Papa God first, Man next, Tiger last.'"

Tiger growled and roared. He let out a low whistle. A band of tigers came running out of the bushes. Tiger said to them, "The man in that tree says: 'Papa God first, Man next, Tiger last'!"

The tigers surrounded the tree, leaping on it, clawing it, shaking it; but tigers can't climb trees, and Man knew this.

"I know what we can do," the first tiger said. "I will lie on the ground and you can climb on my back. We will form a ladder of tigers and the last tiger will be high enough to grab Man."

So Tiger lay down next to the tree, and the tigers, beginning with the heaviest and oldest grandfathers, began to climb on top of him. The last tiger to climb to the top of the pile was the youngest.

As the youngest tiger reached the top, Man leaned over and whispered to him, but loud enough for all the tigers to hear: "If you make one move, I'm going to take out my knife and cut off your head."

Oh! The mother of the baby tiger was in the middle of the pile. When she heard that, she let out such a scream—*YOW*—that all the tigers fell to the ground and ran away.

Then, when they were all gone, Man called out after them, "As I said before: 'Papa God first, Man next, Tiger last'!"

The Last Tiger
in Haiti

The Last Tiger
in Haiti

About the Story: Each time I went to Masson to
hear stories, I was the guest of Bonheur, one of the
hungans of the community. Bonheur was a large,
tall man with a commanding presence and a strong,
forceful voice. He seemed to have incredible en-
ergy. One evening, after four hours of presiding
over the storytelling, he invited Odette and me to a
Voodoo family service for the dead in a clearing in
the woods two miles from the village. The ceremony went on until five in the morning.

During the ceremony, when a participant becomes possessed by a spirit, his face becomes a mask
and he takes on the symbolic and physical qualities
of the spirit. If possessed by Damballah Oueddo,
the snake spirit, he will writhe on the ground and
hiss. In other ceremonies, an animal about to be sac-
rificed will be hypnotized until its eyes and body
reach such a hauntingly human state of tranquility,
that it seems as if it has resigned itself to its fate.
Frequently, after the animal sacrifice, which is done
quickly and with no element of torture, one or
more people will become possessed by a spirit. It
is amazing that often a person who had earlier in the
evening described metamorphoses in stories would,
when undergoing a possession, literally experience
such a transformation.

The Voodoo service for the dead is meant to give the ancestor spirits access to this world through the body of their children so that they can make their wishes known or can offer contact and consolation. But sometimes the spirits come to punish or destroy.

In Bonheur's story, "The Last Tiger in Haiti," the father warns his son about letting "anyone" into the house. The father, a hunter with a secret name, is probably a *hungan*. Bonheur, himself, repeatedly refused the position of *hungan*. His uncle had been a *hungan*, but Bonheur complained that it was too demanding. He already worked during the day as a laborer in the sugar-cane fields. But three years ago when he was twenty-seven, he fell ill. During his sickness, he heard voices and knew he would die if he would not accept the responsibility of *hungan*.

Bonheur and Odette gossipped together during the service, but several times when Bonheur seemed to be paying no attention to the others, he would spring from his seat, crash through the crowd of singing, dancing participants to straighten the upturned skirt of a woman who was possessed or to lift from the ground a man who was undergoing an overwhelming possession. Yet, when Bonheur told stories, I was surprised to see that the audience, who clearly acknowledged him as their religious leader, would, when not enthralled, talk and chatter as freely as if anyone else were speaking. But Bonheur had his tricks: Just when the audience grew restless, he would squat down, his eyes would grow large, and he would introduce some exciting and frightening new event into his stories.

THERE was once a father who had a son. This father was a hunter. He traveled everywhere in Haiti and killed every tiger but one. The one he had not killed was a twisted tiger. After the father killed a tiger he would skin it and wrap its skin very tightly so it looked like a fig. Then he would put it on the balcony to dry.

One day the father told his son, "I am going away. Do not let any of your friends enter the house. And when you are sitting on the balcony do not wave or call to them. But if you should need me, call me by my secret name." The father left.

The boy sat on the balcony. He watched the people walking in the street. He began to feel lonely. Then he saw a friend. He called to him. (It was the last tiger in disguise, but he did not know it.) "*Fssst*. Do you want to come up and visit? I'm alone in the house. Papa has gone away."

"Okay," his friend said.

The boy went down and opened the door. His friend came inside. They went upstairs to the balcony.

The friend would not sit down. He looked at the row of tiger skins on the railing and said, "If you want me to stay with you, give me one of those figs. You have so many."

"Yes, we do have plenty of figs. You can have one."

The boy handed his friend the tiger's skin.

But the moment the friend took the skin he touched it to his heart and he became a living tiger and spoke to the boy: "Your father ate my father, your father ate my mother and my godmother and all my family. Count for me. Count—"

The boy, seeing it was a real tiger, began to cry, "Oh-oh . . . oh—"

"You don't need to cry," said the tiger. "You need to drop all the tiger skins from the balcony to the ground. The skins will become tigers again and they will eat you. Now do as I say."

The boy threw the tiger skins to the ground. He counted:

"One . . . two . . . . three . . . . . four . . . . . . five—"

Then he remembered his father's name, Yaya. He called out: "Yaya, Yaya, poor Franchile."

The father heard him. "What did I tell that boy? I told him not to let his friends enter the house." Still, he called to his son: "Franchile, give out the tiger skins. Count them out, but count them out slowly, very slowly, so I will have time to get home."

When the boy heard this message from his father, he wiped his forehead. He felt a little better.

Now the living tiger called to the boy: "You are giving me tigers from all over the country. I want my *own* relatives now—*my* father, *my* mother, *my* cousins—"

Franchile threw him more tiger skins. He counted them slowly: "Six . . . . . . seven"—he waited a long time—"eight"—he was not going fast—"nine—"

The father came home. He quietly slipped onto the balcony through a small hole. "My child," he whispered, "show me the wicked one, the one who posed as your friend, that one is the only real one."

"There he is, Papa. You see him? The one who is moving."

The father took aim. He shot him. *Pow.* Then all the others dropped to the ground and became tiger skins.

And since that time, there have not been any more tigers in Haiti.

"Bye-Bye"

"Bye-Bye"

About the Story: Michelle was a girl of about nineteen who worked as a seamstress. Sitting on a chair on Jeanne Philippe's porch, she spoke simply and quietly, with a constant twinkle in her eye. When the turtle in the story spoke "the one English word he knew," Michelle looked directly at me, said "Bye-Bye," and burst out laughing. "Bye-Bye!" "Bye-Bye!" the others joined in. There was general merriment. Not until later did I get to hear the end of the story, for everyone wanted at that moment to try out their English words on the American— the one from New York.

ALL the birds were flying from Haiti to New York. But Turtle could not go, for he had no wings.

Pigeon felt sorry for Turtle and said, "Turtle, I'll take you with me. This is what we'll do. I'll hold in my mouth one end of a piece of wood and you hold on to the other end. But you must not let go. No matter what happens, do not let go or you'll fall into the water."

Pigeon took one end of a piece of wood and Turtle the other end. Up into the air Pigeon flew and Turtle with him, across the land and toward the sea.

Elsa Henriquez

As they came near the ocean, Turtle and Pigeon saw on the shore a group of animals who had gathered together to wave good-bye to the birds who were leaving. They were waving steadily until they noticed Turtle and Pigeon. Turtle? They stopped waving and a great hubbub broke out.

"Look!" they cried to each other. "Turtle is going to New York. Even Turtle is going to New York!"

And Turtle was so pleased to hear everyone talking about him that he called out the one English word he knew:

"Bye-Bye!"

Oh-oh. Turtle had opened his mouth, and in opening his mouth to speak, he let go of the piece of wood and fell into the sea.

For that reason there are many Pigeons in New York, but Turtle is still in Haiti.

Songs in English and Creole

The Creole songs appear as transcribed directly from the Haitian singer. The words in these songs which the Haitians say "don't mean anything" can be of French, Spanish, African, Carib-Indian, or early Creole origin. The English translation is sometimes free, otherwise fairly strict, depending on the words and melody. In the cases where no one could offer any translation of the words, such as "Owl," there is only a Haitian version.

from "The Magic Orange Tree"

ENGLISH

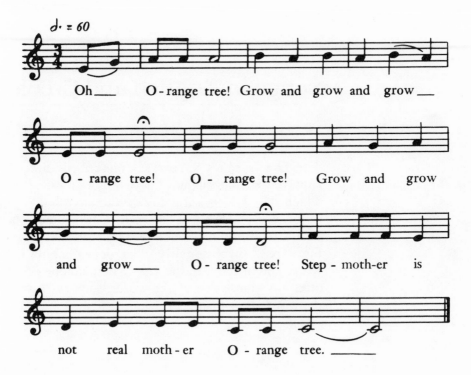

Oh___ O-range tree! Grow and grow and grow___

O - range tree! O - range tree! Grow and grow

and grow___ O - range tree! Step - moth-er is

not real moth - er O - range tree. _____

CREOLE

Ah___ Z'o-range moin pous - sé pous - sé pous - sé

Z'o - range moin Z'o - range moin pous - sé pous -

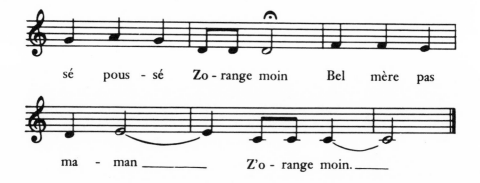

sé   pous - sé   **Zo** - range moin   Bel   mère   pas

ma   –   man _____   Z'o - range moin. _____

from "Owl"

CREOLE

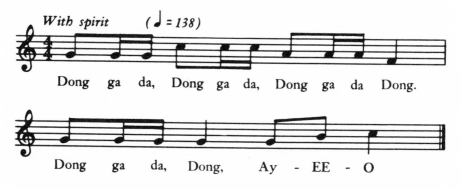

Dong   ga   da,   Dong   ga   da,   Dong   ga   da   Dong.

Dong   ga   da,   Dong,   Ay   -   EE   -   O

THE MAGIC ORANGE TREE

from "Tayzanne"

ENGLISH

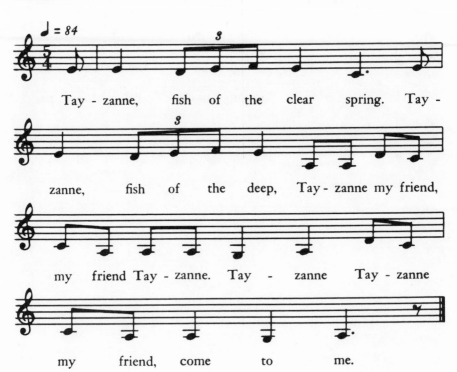

Tay - zanne, fish of the clear spring. Tay -

zanne, fish of the deep, Tay - zanne my friend,

my friend Tay - zanne. Tay - zanne Tay - zanne

my friend, come to me.

CREOLE

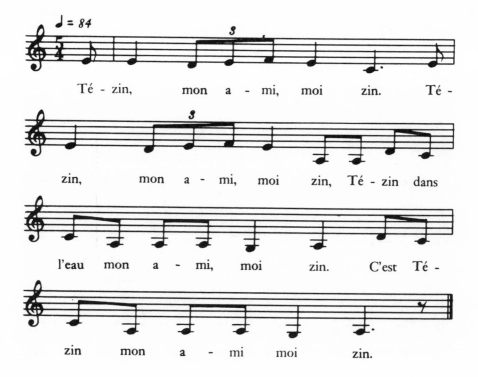

Té - zin, mon a - mi, moi zin. Té -

zin, mon a - mi, moi zin, Té - zin dans

l'eau mon a - mi, moi zin. C'est Té -

zin mon a - mi moi zin.

THE MAGIC ORANGE TREE

from "Bouki Dances the Kokioko"

ENGLISH

♩ = 80 *(ad lib)*

Ko - ki - o - ko oh Sam - ba.

Now I dance, now I dance like this. ____ Ko- ki - o -

ko Oh, Sam - ba. Now I dance, now I dance,

like this. ____ Sam - ba, ____ oh _____

_____ Sam - ba, ah _____ Sam-ba

accelerando

dance, Sam-ba dance, Sam-ba dance, Sam-ba dance Sam-ba
(CLAP)   (CLAP)   (CLAP)   (CLAP)

dance, Sam- ba dance, Sam- ba dance, Sam- ba dance.
(CLAP)   (CLAP)   (CLAP)   (CLAP)

CREOLE

(continuation of song)

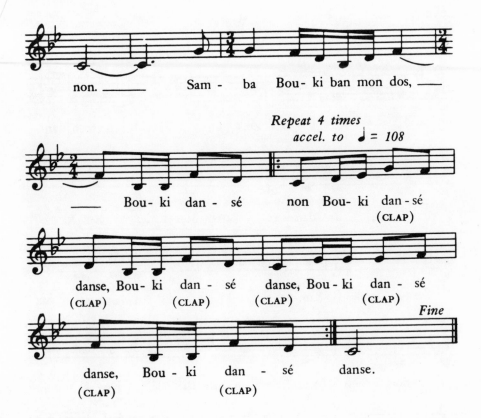

ENGLISH

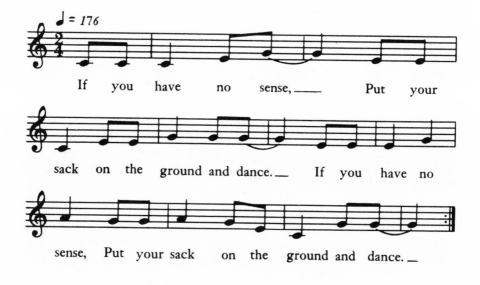

CREOLE

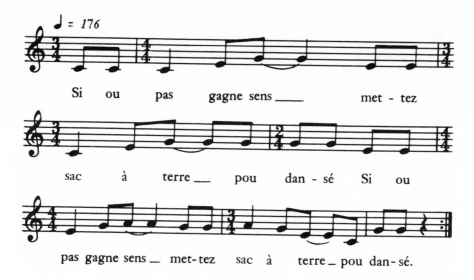

THE MAGIC ORANGE TREE

from "The Singing Bone"

ENGLISH

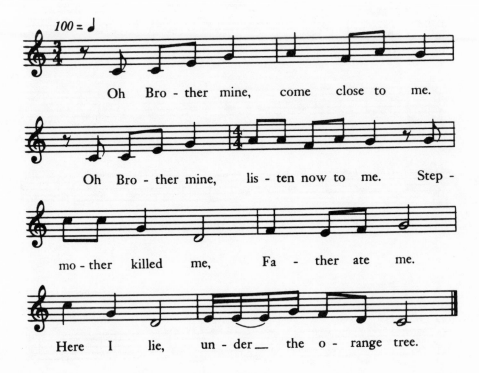

Oh Bro - ther mine, come close to me.

Oh Bro - ther mine, lis - ten now to me. Step -

mo - ther killed me, Fa - ther ate me.

Here I lie, un - der the o - range tree.

CREOLE

Pas - sé,   pas - sé,   c'est mon grand frère moin.

Pas - sé pas - sé,   c'est mon grand frère moin.   Ma

mère qui m'a tué m   mon frè - re m'em por-tém,   Mon

pè - re   qui   m'a   man - gé___   bas   les   o -

range. Pas- sé,   pas - sé,   Dé - ver seau chè - che les bois

li   joinn' les   os   tout d'é   -   zos - sés.

THE MAGIC ORANGE TREE

from "Horse and Toad"

CREOLE

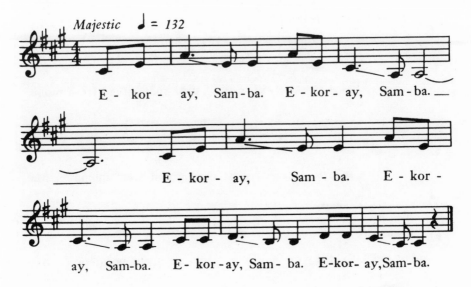

Majestic ♩ = 132

E - kor - ay, Sam - ba. E - kor - ay, Sam - ba. ___

___ E - kor - ay, Sam - ba. E - kor -

ay, Sam-ba. E- kor - ay, Sam - ba. E-kor- ay, Sam-ba.

ENGLISH

Lively ♩ = 152

Tell me, Tell me, Tell me tell me

O tell me true, How can a ti - ny lit - tle

toad like me Win a love-ly girl like you?

CREOLE

Lively ♩ = 120

Com - ment, com - ment, com - ment, com - ment

lan mi - tan mwrin tiou - lé _____ Com -

ment, com - ment com - ment, com - ment lan mi - tan mwrin

tiou - lé _____ cra - paud pi - ti pi - ti con ça

O lan mi - tan mwrin tiou - lé. ___

from "One, My Darling, Come to Mama"

ENGLISH

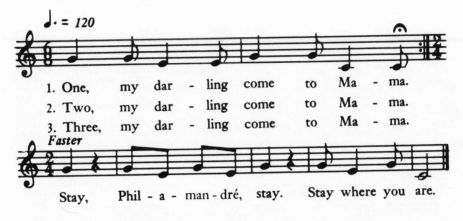

1. One, my dar - ling come to Ma - ma.
2. Two, my dar - ling come to Ma - ma.
3. Three, my dar - ling come to Ma - ma.

Faster

Stay, Phil - a - man - dré, stay. Stay where you are.

---

from "The Forbidden Apple"

ENGLISH

Pa - pa it's not me, it's Lé - on. Nor is it

Bon Ba - zie, it's Lé - on. But e - ven if he's the

one, he's your on - ly son. But e - ven if he's the

one,   he's   your   on - ly   son. ____

CREOLE

Bel   chèr   pa - pa   c'est pas   moin c'est Lé - on. ____

Bel   chèr   pa - pa   c'est pas   moin c'est Lé - on.

C'est pas moin qui - fait   ça,   C'est Lé - on qui - fait ça,

C'est pas   moin qui - fait   ça.   C'est Lé - on qui- fait ça.

Jnou   vie   p' - ti p' - ti   con - ça,

C'est   pas   moin   qui - fait   ça.   ça. ____

My Thanks
and My Love

First to Benjamin Zucker, lover of stories and story-teller, who in his love each time encouraged me to "go to Haiti and *come back!*"

To Jinx Roosevelt and Brooke Goffstein, my muses in the early stages of collecting the stories. Jinx and her children, Amie, Phoebe, and Nick, eagerly came to hear *Cric? Crac!* each time I returned from Haiti. Brooke read the printed versions and said: "Bon Bagaye!"

To Pat Ross, a special editor, who helped me in every way and loved the stories so much that she herself went to Haiti.

To my friends who read the manuscript and whose questions and suggestions greatly added to the content and style of the notes: Joan Bodger, John Flattau, Beebee Gray, Wendy Kesselman, Judith Kroll, Thomas Powers, Lili Seggos, and Erlo Van Waveren.

To Shirley Keller, my friend and a fine musician, who accompanied Rachel and me on our last trip to Haiti and heroically transcribed the Haitian songs and set them in meter and melody.

To Odette Mennesson Riguad and Milo Rigaud, who introduced me to Haiti and critically and encouragingly went over the finished manuscript and illustrations. To Gerald Murray, professor of anthropology at the University of Massachusetts, who suggested themes for the notes and modified my bald statements.

To our daughter, Rachel Cloudstone Zucker, who knows every story in the collection and says, "Cric? Cric? Crack a joke!"

We all love Elsa Henriquez's illustrations.